Time for Snails and Painting Whales

Time for Snails and Painting Whales

Vivien Cooley

MOODY PRESS

CHICAGO

Illustrations by Mark Aydelotte

Library of Congress Cataloguing in Publication Data

Cooley, Vivien, 1951-
    Time for snails and painting whales.

    1. Child rearing—Religious aspects—Christianity.
I. Title.
HQ769.3.C66 1987   261.8′35874   87-24019
ISBN 0-8024-8596-0

2 3 4 5 6 7 Printing/VP/Year 92 91 90 89 88

Printed in the United States of America

*In memory of Dad, who always took
time to listen and encourage—and to
Mom for continuing*

Contents

A TIME TO AFFIRM

Introduction

It has been a tiring afternoon. A mother flops into the closest chair and gazes out the window at her little munchkins at play. As she watches, she is reminded of how precious and short time is with them; how each child needs personal time with her every day, even if it's only a few minutes. But somehow the hectic pace of her life has once again taken over. That isn't what she wants, so she sits up with new resolve. Nothing is going to interfere with that individual time with them. She is willing to rearrange her schedule of housework, job, grocery shopping, church activities, appointments, friendships, and the like. It's a top priority, and it's going to be quality time.

If that sounds somewhat familiar, welcome to the club! We parents are continually struggling with our priorities in relationship to our children, yet God has placed in us the desire to be with them and the understanding that personal time with them is not only important but necessary.

Ecclesiastes 3:1 tells us,

> There is an appointed time for everything.
> And there is a time for every event
> under heaven.

This verse says to us parents that the time to spend with our children is now, while we have them—concentrated time set apart, with our undivided attention, which builds and reinforces each child's self-worth. Our interest says to him, "I want to be with you because I love you. I have fun with you. You are a joy to me."

This is time in which we put aside all distracting thoughts and focus on him. Then we will be affirming him.

What is affirmative time? It's reading a book together, playing with play dough, or going somewhere special; using a chosen activity to generate opportunities for sharing, listening, and fun. Through the following pages you will be given specific ideas in family devotions, art, science, cooking, puppetry, indoor and outdoor creative play, and much more. Each idea is provided as a basis for quality time with your child. You might choose a specific art activity to do together. Tell him what a terrific painter he is and what good ideas he has. Talk about what *he* is interested in. Let him talk with you about what is important to him.

It's quite sobering to realize we have only five years to share with our child without strong outside influences—a short, five-year journey in which we have the opportunity to build a loving, secure relationship; a journey that can create the necessary foundation needed for confidence, strength of character, and a positive lifelong relationship with us.

So often we are in a hurry to have our children grow up. We look to what they will do next rather than savor each moment. The activities provided in this book are designed to enrich today's journey. They will give you a meeting place, a common ground, where you can participate, listen, and affirm.

The result? Your child's self-esteem will be strengthened and his character further molded through your tender direction.

You will find yourself growing more sensitive to him as he teaches you about his world. By listening with the heart, you become a nurturer. Your relationship will be strengthened as he feels accepted and secure.

As a preschool and primary school teacher, I was usually able to pick out those children who were receiving special concentrated time at home. The children were confident, well-adjusted individuals who were sensitive to others' feelings as well as being generally helpful to adults and peers. Since our children spend most of their childhood in schools mastering basic academic skills, it makes sense that we parents need to focus on building in our children what can be properly nourished only through the home: character, self-worth, faith in God, and values.

By nature the activities ahead are educationally enriching, but that is the by-product of affirmative time, not the purpose. Through shared activities you will greatly enrich your lives together today, and you will have built a solid mental, emotional, and spiritual foundation for your child that will last a lifetime.

A TIME TO BEGIN

1
Start When They're Babes

Of course it isn't possible to hold and love your baby all day long! So for those times when she is sitting in an infant seat or lying in her crib, here are a few loving things you can still do for her.

-For the newborn, use a paper plate or cut out a circle. Draw eyes, nose, and smile on it to dangle over the crib or next to the infant seat.

-Hang a soft, sponge dishmop, pie plate, or brightly colored cloth ball over the crib or changing table for the baby to bat at. Be sure to secure objects well.*

-Put bright wrapping paper with interesting designs, bows, Christmas ornaments, cards, or magazine pictures next to the changing table, on kitchen cupboards, or wherever the infant seat is. (Babies really respond to pictures of faces.)

-Mobiles are great, but there are very few made for the *baby* to enjoy. You can make one with bright colored objects, tiny stuffed toys, or colorful wrapping paper glued to cardboard. Hang them so that the objects are looking down at your baby. Attach the objects to the ceiling with fishing line and far enough away so that your baby cannot bat them. A coat hanger can also be used as a base to attach the objects.*

-Get a long, rectangular mirror to attach to the bottom of the wall nearest the floor. Babies love to lie on their tummies and smile at their images. Watch out for any sharp edges.

-In the car, tape colorful wrapping paper, Christmas ornaments, or magazine pictures of faces, children, or animals near the car seat, but far enough away from tiny hands.

-Sew an elastic strip, flat plastic loop, and other safe, soft, flat objects onto a pot holder. Secure each item well. Attach the pot holder to the car seat front with ties for the baby to play with as a cloth activity box.*

*Check frequently to insure objects are still well secured.

A TIME FOR WORSHIP

And you shall love the Lord your God with all your heart and with all your soul and with all your might.

And these words, which I am commanding you today, shall be on your heart;

And you shall teach them diligently to your sons and shall talk of them when you sit in your house and when you walk by the way and when you lie down and when you rise up.

And you shall bind them as a sign on your hand and they shall be as frontals on your forehead.

And you shall write them on the doorposts of your house and on your gates.

(Deuteronomy 6:5-9)

2
Fostering an Awareness of God

When spending quality time with your child, you are not only affirming her in your parent-child relationship, but you are also increasing her awareness of God's affirming love toward her. As a young child, she is seeing Him through your eyes.

The creative activities ahead provide ample opportunities to increase that awareness. While painting, you might talk about God's making each color special for her to enjoy. While banging on rhythm instruments, explain that He has given us many types of music and sound. Thank God out loud and tell Him together how you feel. Pray freely during activities without closing your eyes or folding your hands. Each time, you'll help her understand and sense God's presence and interest in her play. God's touch is everywhere. All that's necessary is *your* being aware of His part in your daily life and allowing your child to see and experience it with you.

HELPING YOUR CHILD PRAY

-Modeling a prayerful life is the best way to help your child learn about prayer. Let him see you praying silently and aloud. Let him see you reading God's Word.

-Have spontaneous prayer. When you're playing or walking, thank God out loud for the lovely day or for legs that enable you to walk. If your pet is sick or someone gets hurt, pray at that time.

-Have regular prayer times before meals and at bedtime. Help your little one to think of things he is thankful for. When he understands that concept, help him think of individuals who need his prayers.

-Have each member of the family pray a one-sentence prayer at bedtime.

-Be sure to emphasize how God has answered your child's specific request right after it is answered. Then thank God together.

-If you are feeling remorseful for the impatience you've shown all morning, apologize to your child, and out loud ask God to forgive you. You may be surprised to find your child praying right along with you!

With the loving, daily outflowing of your relationship with God, your child will see that your heavenly Father is in every aspect of your day, and his, and will find prayer a natural part of living.

DEVOTIONS FOR LITTLE ONES

"Come on, Daddy—and bring the book!" you might hear your preschooler say as he calls out from his bed. He's ready to do devotions. It may have felt awkward at first reading aloud from a children's devotional book, but it became much easier, and now it's an expected part of bedtime!

Preschoolers need routine they can count on, and devotions can be a meaningful, tender "routine" that they quickly grow to love. It doesn't have to be at bedtime. During or after dinner, after bath, or even every other day is fine. It just needs to be as consistent as possible.

Devotions enable you to set an example of worship and of learning about God. They provide an enjoyable time of sharing together in an atmosphere of love, safety, and unity. And they help you build in your children a foundation of belief and trust in God, of worship, and of the importance of God's Word to our daily lives.

What a precious privilege to speak of Christ with your little ones and to set a daily pattern for God's Word that one day they will continue to follow on their own.

In laying a firm foundation in Christ for your child, there are two things to keep in mind. The first is that even if you're one to be consistent in your own personal devotional time, it will take discipline on your part to make sure that family devotions consistently take place.

The second is that your child's image and understanding of God's character is a direct reflection of what his relationship is with you. If you are accepting of physical, mental, or emotional limitations due to age or a handicap, he will view God as accepting him. If you are a praising parent, who also listens and forgives, he will see God that way.

You are a wonderful tool that God is using as the greatest influence in your child's life. I wish you all the joy and pleasure that family devotions can bring.

Here are a few guidelines to help you get started:

-Try to set a definite time to do devotions each day. If schedules absolutely don't permit, do them when you can. Sometimes is better than never.

-Try to keep things as simple as possible, keeping explanations short.

-Due to the short attention span of preschoolers, it is a good idea for devotion time to last no more than five to seven minutes.

-Rotate any of the books and ideas to follow in order to create fresh interest each devotion time.

-Have you seen the wonderful children's Bibles available for preschoolers? They are appealing and easy to understand (see Resources).

-You know you child best. If he just isn't interested in what you've planned, then change pace. Have him choose a favorite story book. Whether it's Christian or secular, you can usually make a biblical application.

-It's important to keep in mind that children need concrete explanations and examples in order to grasp meanings, otherwise they tend to take abstract concepts (such as "Jesus is the light of the world") literally. Instead, try to teach concrete concepts: that Jesus loves them and wants to be their best friend, and that He is God's holy Son. There will be plenty of opportunity for them to learn abstract concepts when their young minds have sufficiently matured.

-Close with one simple verse and a prayer. Using a Bible verse each time gives the child the sense that God's Word is important and can guide us in all that we do. Mark the verse ahead of time for easy access.

-One way to have prayer is for each family member to say a sentence prayer. This often helps prechoolers overcome hesitancy in praying aloud and creates a family unity in prayer.

Some Ideas for Devotions*

-Dinnertime is a good time to focus on a character quality and its application and meaning. Why not take one character quality a week:

- What is patience? Kindness? Thoughtfulness? Generosity?
- Think of practical ways to show that quality in your home, with friends, pets, etc.

*Many thanks to Judy Wortley for her faithful, creative, and encouraging input into this section.

- Praise the quality as you see it displayed in their lives.
- Read a simple Bible verse that you can all learn together.
- End with prayer.

-Start the morning with a greeting toward the Lord. "Hey, I wonder what God has for you today?" "Look at the rain God has brought us!" This helps the child's first thoughts each day, and the first words he hears, to be directed toward the Lord.

-There are children's character-building stories available on sharing, helping, forgiving, and so on. Many come with tapes. Some of these, which come in a series, are Ethel Barrett's *Communicating Christian Values to Children, Critter County Storytime, David and I Talk to God,* based on the Psalms, and *God's Word in My Heart.* These are excellent springboards for discussion. End with prayer on the focused concept.

-Play children's Christian albums (see Resources), and use rhythm instruments with them. Read Psalm 147:1*a.* "Praise the Lord! For it is good to sing praises to our God." End with sentence prayer thanking God for music and for ears to hear.

-Read a page from *The Bible Illustrated for Little Children* or *My Picture Bible to See and Share.* In both books, each page focuses on a one-paragraph Bible story and has two or three questions to ask. These particular books illustrate Jesus' death on the cross in an appropriate manner for preschoolers. Both show Jesus on the cross from behind, so that the child doesn't see Jesus beaten and suffering. This is important because little children's concept of our Lord is forming. They can know He died for them, but it isn't necessary for them to see such vivid pictures until they can emotionally handle them.

-Try *Big Thoughts for Little People.* This book teaches children positive Christian values by applying them to each letter of the alphabet. *F* is for forgive, *J* is for joyful, *P* is for polite. It also deals with the negatives; *C* is for crying, *L* is for lying. The illustrations are involving, and each page has at least one ladybug to find. There are two or three questions about each picture to help make the applications personal.

-How about trying *Christian Nursery Rhymes?* The author has adapted familiar nursery rhymes by changing several lines in each to make them God-centered. These would be fun to memorize.

-Play preschool Bible games available in Bible bookstores. You will find matching games for Bible animals, children, and stories, as well as Lotto games, jigsaw puzzles, and lacing cards. Be sure to end with prayer as a focus time.

-Make a sticker prayer list. List each item that your child wants to pray for (draw pictures next to the written word so that your child can "read" the list too). As the prayers are answered, the child puts a sticker next to the request. This will enable him to see in a concrete way that God does answer prayer. Children have a wonderful way of thanking God more than requesting. To keep that perspective, it's a good idea to also emphasize what he is thankful for.

-Read a Happy Day book from Standard Publishing Company. One such story is *How God Gives Us Peanut Butter.* After reading it, make peanut butter cookies or a peanut butter sandwich. Then thank God for peanut butter! Another is *Jesus Loves Me All the Time.* Draw a picture of your favorite activity and write below it, "Jesus loves me when I . . ."

-*The Good Night Book, The Sleep Tight Book,* and *Before You Tuck Me In* are all short readings for young children, covering all sorts of subjects children find interesting. It seems that most of the readings are for ages six through eight, but preschoolers still enjoy them. If you have a preschooler and a primary age child, these books would be ideal.

-Eat pancakes for dinner and then make a pancake book. Have precut pancake-shaped paper for each member of the family (along with precut front and back cover). Everyone draws his favorite kind of pancake (buckwheat, blueberry, whole wheat, etc.). Most preschoolers will simply scribble, but that is their important contribution! Staple the pictures together inside the covers. You might write, "Thank You, God, for Pancakes," or, "God Gives Us Good Food," on the cover.

-You can make any kind of book on any kind of subject. For example, if you've just had a fun family outing, have each person draw his favorite part of the experience. Encourage each child to dictate a sentence for you to write at the bottom of his page, or let him "write" his own. Staple together. Put a thought concerning the Lord or a Bible verse on the cover and put on the coffee table for all to enjoy.

-Have a song fest! You may not know many or any songs for children, but don't be discouraged. There are terrific children's songs on tapes and records that you can learn right along with your child. (See Resources.)

-You might draw a picture of something you are afraid of. Draw yourself in the picture. Then draw Jesus in between you and what you're afraid of. Put into a family book with an appropriate verse on the cover and leave on the coffee table, or give it to a hospitalized friend as a reminder that Jesus is right there with him.

-Read together any Sunday school papers sent home. Usually there is a Bible story emphasized and/or a children's story with a biblical application. This is also good for reinforcing what the child has just learned that morning at church.

A TIME TO CREATE

3
Art

You can expect your very young child to be interested only momentarily in poking at play dough, painting, or gluing until she reaches age three or four. Don't let that discourage you. No matter how short her attention span, you are spending precious time together!

The art activities in this book are divided into four main categories: painting, cutting and gluing, hats, and miscellaneous messes. These are followed by chapters on seasonal art activities and recipes for paint and play dough, with some extra art recipes. Almost all of the activities require things you already have at home.

YOU CAN BE MOST HELPFUL TO YOUR CHILD BY REMEMBERING TO:

-Praise, praise, praise her efforts!

-Be patient and don't rush her. Pick a time when you can relax.

-Then relax some more—messes are going to occur!

-Say, "Tell me about your picture," or, "Tell me about what you're making," rather than, "What is it?"

-Be sure to show pride in your child's efforts by hanging up her work. An art box for artwork gathered at home and church can alleviate the problem of too many pictures or projects at one time and still express that you value the work. After a few weeks, you can go through the box and keep those papers that are special. Mail a picture to grandma, uncle, or a sick friend.

DID YOU KNOW?

Besides being lots of fun, art

-encourages self-expression (there are no "wrong" answers or conclusions)

-encourages creativity

-develops eye-hand coordination

-develops fine motor control (through scissors, crayons, hole-punch, lacing with needle and thread)

-develops large motor control (through large movements as when painting on a large surface)

-develops a sense of color and texture

-develops a sense of pride in beginning and completing a task (even though the completing is child-determined)

-develops attentiveness to a task

-provides experiences in various art media (watercolor, tempera, collage, gluing, lacing, weaving)

If your child doesn't seem to be interested in art right now, don't be concerned. Most children enjoy art, but a child's desire is less if he'd rather be playing outdoors or if he is already experiencing art in a school setting. Instead, join him in what *he* wants to do.

SUGGESTED BASIC SUPPLIES

Here are a few basic art supplies that are helpful to have on hand:

-Red, yellow, and blue tempera paint (powdered or liquid). These can be purchased at art, hobby, or school supply stores. Mix these three primary colors to make other colors:

red+blue=purple
red+yellow=orange
blue+yellow=green

-Liquid starch. A squirt of starch added to a small blob of paint acts as an extender and saves you money. Add a dab of dishwashing liquid to starch and paint mixture to make clothes and hands easier to clean.

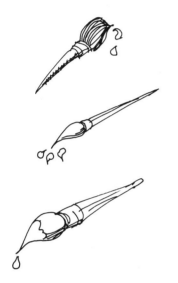

-Box of crayons

-Three or more paint brushes of varying widths from art, hobby, or paint stores

-Butcher paper. Newsprint can be purchased in a roll at your local newspaper for a dollar or more, depending on the amount of paper you want. (You are buying the end of a roll that the newspress no longer needs.)

-Tablet of construction paper purchased at drug, art, or hobby stores

-Yogurt, margarine, or whipped topping containers (save lids!) for storing paint

-Plastic tub

-Old T-shirt for paint shirt

-Bottle of glue

-Old plastic tablecloth for a tarp

-Food coloring

-Save old ribbons, lace, plastic flowers, buttons, gift wrap, wallpaper, toilet paper tubes. Nothing is useless when it comes to art!

-You may want to add to this list as your budget allows—watercolors, colored tissue paper, glitter, and so on.

4
Painting Activities

PAINTING BOXES

Supplies needed:
- paint
- paint containers
- brushes
- any size box

Watch your child have fun painting on the inside and outside of a box! The larger the box the better. Crayons and felt pens are fine too.

SAND PAINTING

Supplies needed:
- construction paper or butcher paper
- bottle of glue
- sand or dirt
- powdered tempera paint

Draw a picture by squirting glue all over a piece of paper. Cover the picture with sand, and when sand is shaken off—surprise! An entirely different picture emerges. Let dry well before displaying since glue can drip. For colored sand, mix powered tempera paint with sand and keep in container or shaker.

WATER PAINTING

Supplies needed:
- paint brush
- container of water

On a hot day, it's wonderful to "paint" a picture on the sidewalk or on the side of your house with harmless water. Within minutes the painting has evaporated and a new one can be made!

DRIP PICTURES

Supplies needed:
- paint
- brushes
- paper

Dab paint along the edge of one side of the paper. Hold it up to let paint drip down and around. Then put colors on another edge and do the same until all four sides are drip-painted.

ICE CUBE PAINTING

Supplies needed:
- paint
- ice cube tray
- piece of paper (the larger the better)

Pour liquid tempera paint of various colors into an ice cube tray and freeze. When frozen, use like crayons. Messy but fun.

ROLL-ON PAINTING

Supplies needed:
- empty roll-on deodorant containers
- paint
- paper
- liquid starch

This is a fun project, and family friends can help you save the containers. Take the plastic ball and cap off the bottles. After cleaning well, fill with paint. Add a little starch as an extender and for smoothness. Replace ball and cap and have fun.

FINGER PAINTING

Supplies needed:
 paper
 paint
 roasting pan or cookie sheet

Put paper in bottom of pan or cookie sheet. The paint is less apt to get all over. Put different blobs of paint onto the paper and paint with your hands. Liquid starch can be added as an extender.

TABLE FINGER PAINTING

Supplies needed:
 paint
 paper
 a child's table or other easily-washed-off surface

The difference in table finger painting is that the paint is put directly onto the table surface. When child is done painting, lay paper on top of the designs made and press. When paper is lifted up, the designs are transferred onto the paper. Starch can be used to extend.

STRING PAINTING

Supplies needed:
 string about 12″ long
 paint
 containers for paint
 paper

Put a piece of string into each container of paint. Swirl each string around the paper, making interesting designs. (If paint is too thick, use less paint and add liquid starch.)

GLITTER PAINTING

Supplies needed:
 glitter
 paint
 containers for paint
 paper
 brushes

Mix glitter and paint and watch the sparkly results as you paint a picture.

FOOTSIE HANGING

Supplies needed:
 paint
 cookie sheet
 large piece of paper (butcher paper is best)
 tub of water
 towel

Pour paint onto cookie sheet, and place the paper in front of the cookie sheet. Place tub of water and a towel at the other end of paper. The child, with parent helping steady him, steps into the cookie sheet, getting paint all over the soles of his feet. He then walks all over the paper. When done, he simply walks to the tub of water and washes his feet. Then it's Mom or Dad's turn!

SPONGE PRINTS

Supplies needed:
 sponge (synthetic, flat sponge works best)
 scissors
 containers for paint
 paint
 paper

Cut various shapes, animals, people, out of sponge. Fill containers shallowly with paint. Dab sponge shapes in paint and print onto paper.

COOKIE CUTTER PRINTS

Supplies needed:
 cookie cutters
 paint
 paper
 containers for paints

Just as for the sponge prints, cookie cutters can be used. Potatoes can also be carved and used in this activity.

GADGET PAINTING

Supplies needed:
  paint
  paper
  containers for paint
  kitchen gadgets
The same technique is used as with sponge and cookie cutter printing.

ANYTHING PAINTING

Supplies needed:
  paper (any of the following: construction paper, cardboard, sandpaper, gift wrap, butcher, shelf, newspaper, wallpaper, paper bags, corrugated)
  paint
  containers for paint
  anything you can think of to paint with
Paint with feathers, forks, cotton balls, Q-tips, old toothbrushes, strawberry baskets, combs, string, or crunched-up paper wads!

MARBLE PAINTING

Supplies needed:
  a flat box or box lid or metal cake pan
  paper
  marbles
  small containers of paint
  spoons
Place a sheet of paper in bottom of box. Put a marble in each container of paint. Scoop marble up with spoon and place marble in box. Pick up box and roll marble all over paper. Then do the same with other colors.

PAINT TO MUSIC

Supplies needed:
  paint, crayons, or felt pens
  paper (preferably a large piece)
  paint brushes
  music
Play a slow song and paint slowly. Play a fast song and paint fast. How does the music make you feel? How does it make your arm feel? See what pretty designs you can make.

COLORED CHALK PAINTING

Supplies needed:
  colored chalk
  cup of water or a blob of buttermilk
  paper
Dip chalk into water or buttermilk and draw on paper. The water and milk both bring out the colors, making them brighter and more permanent.

NOTHING IN PARTICULAR

Supplies needed:
  large piece of paper, newspaper, or wallpaper
  crayons, felt pens, or paint
  paint brushes
Just put out a piece of paper and lie there painting, coloring, or drawing together!

PUDDING PAINTING

Supplies needed:
  instant chocolate pudding
  milk
  mixer
  bowl
  measuring cup
  paper
  table with an easy-wipe-off surface
Make a small package of chocolate pudding according to package directions. Put some directly onto table surface. Swirl all over the table. Make designs and pictures. When done, just as in table finger painting, press paper over design to preserve the masterpiece. Eat whatever pudding is left in the bowl! This is one project where little hands and table need to be extra clean before starting.

WATERCOLORS

Supplies needed:
  watercolor set
  paper
  container of water
Children love to see watercolors react to

31

paper and choose which color from the tray they want to use next.

Supplies needed:
    paint
    construction paper
    brush

Fold the paper in half, and open it up again. Paint on only one of the folded sides. When done, fold paper in half again, and press. Open it to see what design, pattern, or animal was made.

FUZZ PAINTING

Supplies needed:
    paint (food coloring diluted in water
      can be substituted)
    paper
    paint brush
    tub of water

Wet paper thoroughly in a tub of water. Hold paper by one corner while child dabs paint in corner that is being held. Watch as paint fuzzes. Add another color to the same corner. Watch as colors blend to make a new color. Keep adding colors until paint stops fuzzing. Let dry.

GOOP

Supplies needed:
    food coloring
    squirt bottles (ketchup bottles or those
      used for permanents from beauty
      supply stores are good)
    equal parts of salt, flour, and water

Mix salt, flour, and water together and pour into each squirt bottle. Add a few drops of food coloring or paint to each bottle, replace lid, and shake. Squirt the goop onto paper. Goop makes a wonderful, textured design. When dry, it has a raised, almost sparkly quality from the salt.

STRAW PICTURES

Supplies needed:
    paint
    liquid starch
    drinking straw
    paper

Add squirt of starch to paint to act as a diluter and extender. Put a small dab of paint onto paper and blow paint in different directions with straw. It's tiring, but fun! Add glitter if desired.

CHALK

Supplies needed:
    colored chalk
    small container of water or buttermilk
    paper, wallpaper, or sandpaper

Use chalk on wet paper.
Use chalk on paper on which buttermilk
  has been spread.
Use chalk on sandpaper.

SHAVING CREAM PAINTING

Supplies needed:
    shaving cream (or whipped topping)
    paint
    large piece of paper, preferably butcher
      paper

Spray shaving cream onto paper. Feel, smell, and play with the cream. Sprinkle paint over cream and smear. Add glitter if you have some.

JAR PAINTING

Supplies needed:
    liquid paint
    baby food jars
    rubber bands
    paper

Put a blob of paint on paper. Place rubber bands around jars in askew patterns. Roll the jars through the paint and then onto paper for interesting patterns.

Supplies needed:
    large piece of paper the size of your
        child's body length
    crayons or felt pens
    paint

The child lies on paper while you trace around her. When done, she paints her hair, face, and clothing onto the paper. When dry, cut out and hang on the wall. You can even cut out two of her and stuff with paper to stand in her room.

5
Cutting and Gluing Activities

PAPER STRIP ART

Supplies needed:
> strips of colored construction paper
> glue (squirt glue onto a plastic lid for easy dipping)
> one large piece of construction paper, cardboard, or wood

Children have a grand time making cities, playgrounds, fairs, or whatever with strips of paper. Show your child that he can glue the strip twisted, flat, zig-zag, or on its side. Simply dip each end of the strip into the glue. What can you make, Mom or Dad?

JUNK COLLAGE

Supplies needed:
> paper
> glue
> any junk

Let's face it, anything can be glued for a collage—leaves, styrofoam, rocks, colored tissue, bottle caps, buttons, foil, ribbon, yarn . . .

WOOD SCULPTURE

Supplies needed:
> small wood scraps (obtained from lumber yard)
> glue
> cardboard or wood base
> pie tin or other container for glue dipping

Dip wood scrap into glue and place it on base. Create a space station, city, fort, doll house, or anything. When dry, paint it.

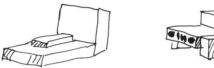

NATURE WALK

Supplies needed:
> glue
> container to collect things in
> piece of paper

Go on a nature walk. Talk about all the things you see that God has made. Collect as many different objects as you can and then come home and glue them onto a piece of paper. You might even want to put at the bottom of the paper, "Things God Has Made."

JIGSAW PUZZLE

Supplies needed:
> a picture from a magazine
> glue
> a thin piece of cardboard
> scissors, ruler, thin felt marker

Choose a picture from a magazine, and glue it onto cardboard piece. When dry, cut off excess cardboard around picture. Using the ruler and pen, divide the picture into four equal parts. Cut up the picture using the pen marks as a guide. Of course, the younger the child, the more help he'll need with this part. He'll have fun putting the puzzle back together again. Make one for a sick friend.

SHAPES PICTURES

Supplies needed:
    colored construction paper precut into
        circles, triangles, squares,
        rectangles, stars, hearts, clovers,
        etc., of varying sizes
    one whole piece of paper
    glue

Make animals, cars, patterns, and designs with the shapes. Glue them onto the construction paper.

MAGAZINE COLLAGE

Supplies needed:
    magazines
    glue
    one piece of construction paper,
        newspaper, or wallpaper
    scissors

Cut out pictures from magazines and glue them onto construction paper. Make it more interesting by giving her a triangle piece of construction paper, or how about a heart?

HOLE-PUNCH PICTURES

Supplies needed:
    hole-punch
    colored constuction paper or
        magazines
    one piece of paper
    bottle of glue

Punch holes in magazines or construction paper with hole punch. Save the holes. Make a picture with the holes by dabbing glue onto the paper with glue bottle or a Q-tip and laying holes on top.

A SPECIAL BOOK

Supplies needed:
    construction paper
    brads or stapler
    magazines or photos
    glue

Your child will enjoy making and reading his own book. Just make a book by stapling or punching holes along one edge of pages and threading with yarn. When your child sees magazine pictures or photos he likes, he can glue them into his book.

CYLINDER JUNK ART

Supplies needed:
    various sizes and lengths of paper
        towel tubes and toilet tissue tubes
    glue—in a pie plate
    piece of stiff paper or cardboard

Dip one end of tube into pan of glue and stick onto cardboard base. Glue tubes at different angles. When dry, paint them, sprinkle glitter, add styrofoam pieces, feathers, and so on. What a masterpiece!

6
Hats, Hats, Hats

Children love wearing hats, and many simple ones can be made with a few strips of paper. Here are just a few:

Supplies needed:
  paper
  stapler or glue
  scissors

Cut two strips of paper and staple together for the base (be sure that staples point away from child's head):

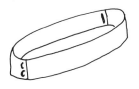

Then cut out two ears, and staple or glue onto base. You can also add smaller pink ears and glue inside the larger ones.

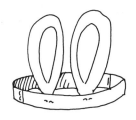

CROWN

Supplies needed:
  paper
  scissors
  stapler or glue
  felt pens, glitter, etc., to decorate

Simply fold a piece of paper in half and cut zig-zag at the fold:

Then staple together at both ends:

You can decorate the crown before or after stapling.

DAVEY CROCKETT HAT

Supplies needed:
  small brown lunch bag
  scissors
  stapler or glue
  black crayon

Cut off the bottom of sack, leaving sides about 2½" to 3":

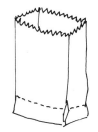

Cut out a tail from leftover sack. Draw "raccoon" stripes on tail. Staple or glue tail to back of hat.

SPACE HELMETS

Supplies needed:
    large grocery bag or cylinder ice cream
      container (the large kind ice cream
      stores have; ask for any they don't
      want or are ready to throw out)
    two pipe cleaners
    felt pens or crayons
    scissors

Cut out a rectangle opening to see through.
Draw knobs or designs on sack and add
antennae.

LET'S GET BUGGY!

Supplies needed:
    one piece of construction paper
    scissors
    two pipe cleaners
    stapler or glue

Make a paper base as done for bunny ears.
Staple pipe cleaners on for antennae. Curl
ends of pipe cleaners for a buggy look!

REINDEER ANTLERS

Supplies needed:
    construction paper
    scissors
    stapler or glue

Make a paper base as done for bunny ears.
Trace around your child's hands on construction paper and cut them out. Staple or
glue onto base. The hands are the antlers!

EASTER BONNET

Supplies needed:
    paper plate
    glue
    yarn
    stapler
    old jewelry, sequins, tissue paper,
      styrofoam squiggles

Glue jewelry and other decorations onto top
of plate. For a tie, cut two strips of yarn
and staple each to opposite edges of plate.

DINOSAUR HAT

Supplies needed:
    construction paper (large)
    stapler
    scissors
    crayon or felt pen

Fold paper in half and draw a stegosaurus
on one side. Cut both out and staple ends
together. Add a face and wear.

7
Miscellaneous Messes

STYROFOAM SCULPTURES

Supplies needed:
> styrofoam squiggles (also known as
>   packing styrofoam)
> toothpicks
> styrofoam meat tray or other flat piece
>   of styrofoam

Simply stick toothpicks into styrofoam tray. Decorate and connect the toothpicks with the small styrofoam pieces.

SEWING

Supplies needed:
> styrofoam meat tray
> large needle
> colored yarn

Thread needle with yarn. Knot the bottom end as usual and tie the other end to the needle's eye. This will prevent yarn from slipping out of the needle. Help your child sew up and down through the meat tray.

WEAVING BASKETS

Supplies needed:
> strawberry basket
> yarn
> small piece of masking tape

Tie one end of yarn to a corner of basket, and wrap tape around the other end to act as a needle. Weave the yarn in and out and around the basket.

BAND-AID COLLAGE

Supplies needed:
> box of Band-Aids
> piece of paper

Most young children need help getting the outer wrapper and end papers off. Place each Band-Aid randomly on the paper as a collage.

WAXED PAPER COLLAGE

Supplies needed:
> waxed paper
> iron
> newspaper
> collage items

Collect leaves or other flat nature items. Lay several layers of newspaper on the table and put one piece of waxed paper on newspaper (waxed side up). Lay the nature items on waxed paper and cover with one more piece of waxed paper (waxed side down). Cover everything with serveral layers of newspaper. With iron on medium heat, iron newspaper, checking carefully to see if waxed paper is fusing together. Trim any rough edges, and hang in window. Crayon shavings of red, orange, and yellow make a fun addition and help the waxed paper fuse better.

CORNSTARCH GOO

Supplies needed:
> one box of cornstarch
> a tub
> water

Dump all of the cornstarch into the tub and add water slowly, constantly stirring. Add just enough water so that the cornstarch, when picked up in the hand and squeezed, becomes immediately hard and then acts as if it's melting through your fingers. This mixture is a fun kind of "mud" to work with your hands.

FOOD COLORING PICTURES

Supplies needed:

    red, blue, and yellow food coloring
    a paper towel (the sturdier the better)
    three containers of water

Fold the paper towel three times, each time making a triangle. Add food coloring to each container of water. Be sure to make the colors strong. Dip each end of triangle in a different color, allowing each color to soak up to the middle of the paper. When the towel is opened, the primary colors blending together will have also made the secondary colors—purple, orange, and green.

ICE CUBE PAINTING

Supplies needed:

    ice cube tray
    water
    eye dropper
    red, blue, and yellow food coloring

Put the three primary colors into three end compartments of the tray, and fill entire tray with water. Use an eye dropper to take color from the end compartments to make new colors in the others.

TISSUE PAPER COLLAGE

Supplies needed:

    liquid starch
    colored tissue paper (torn into small
      pieces)
    brush
    paper

Brush starch onto paper and lay tissue paper over starched areas. Brush more starch over tissue for a finished, glossy product.

STRINGING MACARONI

Supplies needed:

    food coloring
    rubbing alcohol (about ¼ cup per bowl
      of water)
    large size macaroni
    string
    needle
    slotted spoon or colander
    containers of water

Dye macaroni in several bowls of rubbing alcohol and food coloring. Use a slotted spoon to remove macaroni, and lay out on waxed paper or foil to dry. Run your hands over them occasionally to keep them from sticking to the paper. When dry, string them. Store leftovers in a sealed container.

CRAYON RUBS

Supplies needed:

    crayons
    paper

Have your child feel objects such as coins, leaves, wood—anything that has an interesting texture. Feel them with your eyes closed too. Show him how to make a crayon rub by placing paper over each object and rubbing over the area with the side of a crayon. How many objects can each of you find?

RUBBER STAMPS

Supplies needed:

    ink pad (they come in a variety of
      colors)
    paper
    rubber stamps

Rubber stamps are popular and therefore easy to find, from cartoon characters to miscellaneous words to names. Children enjoy stamping pictures onto paper. One idea is to use zoo animal stamps, for example, and using crayons first, draw cages or habitats. When done, stamp in the animals. A jungle scene can also be created.

PLAY DOUGH

With play dough, use rolling pins, cookie cutters, kitchen gadgets with interesting surfaces, and wooden mallets! (See recipes in chap. 9.)

8
Holiday Ideas

VALENTINES DAY

Let your child decorate his room and your house with homemade hearts you've made together! Here are some other things to do for Valentines Day:

VALENTINES WAXED PAPER COLLAGE

Supplies needed:
- waxed paper
- scissors
- iron
- newspaper
- precut hearts and small doilies
- red crayon shavings

Cut two sheets of waxed paper into indentical shapes. Cut out paper hearts and cut doilies into smaller pieces. Follow directions as stated in Waxed Paper Collage (chap. 7), using crayon shavings in the collage.

HEART COOKIES

Supplies needed:
- your favorite sugar cookie recipe
- red or pink frosting (add red food coloring to white frosting)
- sprinkles
- blunt knife
- heart-shaped cookie cutter

Just make and bake cookies according to your recipe. Decorate with frosting and sprinkles. Why not give to a friend to tell him that God loves him and you do too?

WHIPPED FUN

Supplies needed:
- detergent soap flakes (such as Ivory Snow)
- mixer
- red food coloring
- water (enough to make finger-paint consistency)
- paper

Whip water, soap flakes, and food coloring together in mixer to finger-paint consistency and pour some onto paper. It's great fun finger painting with the soft, foamy paint!

MAKE A SPECIAL PLACEMAT

Supplies needed:
- paper
- cut-out hearts, doilies, etc.
- glue

Your child will enjoy eating on a placemat that he has made. Just glue hearts and doilies onto a piece of paper and use. To preserve placemat, cover with clear contact paper. Placemat can also be made with waxed paper as done in Valentine Waxed Paper Collage.

DOILY PAINTING

Supplies needed:
- red and/or pink paint
- brushes
- doilies (small or large)
- construction paper

Lay doily on construction paper and paint

over cut-out areas. Move doily around and paint again. You can decorate paper hearts with doily painting too.

VALENTINE COOKIE CUTTER PRINTS

Supplies needed:
   red, white, or pink paint
   construction paper
   Valentine cookie cutters
   shallow tray for paint

Press cookie cutter in paint and then onto paper. Make interesting designs with your cutters.

VALENTINE CARDS

Supplies needed:
   regular-sized stationery
   Valentine cookie cutter
   paint
   shallow tray for paint
   glitter (optional)

Fold stationery in half to make a card. As in Cookie Cutter Prints, dip cutter into paint tray and then onto stationery. Sprinkle with glitter. Let dry and let child "write" his special Valentine message.

MAILMAN

Supplies needed:
(for mail hat and mailbox) con-	(For mail)
struction paper	old envelopes
contact paper	old cards
string	rubber stamps
colored pens, cray-	and pad
ons, or paint	stickers
glue	old Easter seals
	crayons, pens, etc.

Cut mail hat as shown and attach string for ties. Decorate. For mailbox, wrap shoe box in construction paper or colored contact paper. Cut slit in lid. Decorate if desired. Mail can then be made using the old envelopes and cards.

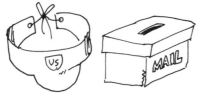

HEART NECKLACES

Supplies needed:
   paint
   brushes
   paper clip
   air-dry play dough (see recipe in chap. 7)

After you've both made the play dough, make hearts using a cookie cutter. Place a paper clip in the back of each dough heart (for a hook), and let dry. Paint and string with yarn for a necklace. Give others to friends to tell them that you love them.

GOOP HEARTS

Supplies needed:
   goop (see recipe in chap. 9)
   paper hearts

Decorate paper hearts with goop in squeeze bottles. Let dry thoroughly. Beauticians will often save permanent wave bottles for you, or bottles can be purchased at beauty supply stores.

SHOW SOMEONE YOU CARE

-Make Valentine cookies for a lonely person, shut-in, Sunday school teacher, or your church custodian. You might want to take fruit for someone recuperating from an illness.

-Send homemade Valentine cards to special people in your life, telling them that God loves them and so do you.

-Make a bird feeder for your garden friends (see chap. 10)

-Do gardening or housework for an elderly person. Your child will enjoy helping and see the appreciation shown by the elderly.

EASTER

TISSUE CROSS

Supplies needed:
   colored construction paper
   colored tissue paper
   liquid starch
   brush

Cut out the shape of a cross and decorate this reminder that our Lord is no longer there! Brush starch onto paper and lay tissue on top. Brush more starch over tissue for finish. Another way is to have your child poke his finger into precut squares of tissue and squeeze the tissue around finger. Then point tissue down onto paper so that it stands up. No starch is needed on top.

PAPER PLATE BUNNIES

Supplies needed:
- two paper plates
- crayons
- scissors and glue
- pipe cleaners or toothpicks

Cut one paper plate in half for the ears and staple onto the whole plate. Decorate face and add pipe cleaners or toothpicks for whiskers. See also chapter 6 for paper plate "Easter Bonnets" and "Bunny Ears".

EASTER EGG COOKIES

Supplies needed:
- your favorite sugar cookie recipe
- frosting
- sprinkles
- blunt knife
- egg-shaped cookie cutter

Make cookies according to your recipe. Decorate with frosting and sprinkles.

STRAWBERRY EASTER BASKETS

Supplies needed:
- strawberry basket
- glue
- scissors
- tissue or colored construction paper
- stapler

Glue precut squares of paper or tissue on outside and/or inside of basket. Use a strip of paper stapled on for handle.

A SPECIAL EASTER STORY

Supplies needed:
- a shoe box or tub
- dirt or sand

toy people you already have at home
a cup (paper or styrofoam is best)
any twigs or pieces of shrubs
a cup-size flat stone

This idea is added because it is a meaningful way of explaining Jesus' resurrection to a young child. Put dirt or sand in box. Place cup on its side in sand (this is the tomb). Put flat stone near entrance to tomb. Place shrubbery around tomb area. Using the people, let one be the angel that brought the good news to the mourners, "Don't be afraid! You don't have to be sad anymore. Jesus isn't in the tomb—He's alive!" Let your children play with the figures. You'll be thrilled to see how real the Easter story becomes as they reenact it over and over.

BLOSSOM BRANCH

Supplies needed:
- a bare branch
- tissue paper
- glue

Dab glue all over branch. Wad up pieces of tissue and place them on glue to look like blossoms—new life!

PLASTIC EGGS

Supplies needed:
- plastic colored eggs
- rick-rack, sequins, or any other trimmings to decorate eggs
- glue

Decorate eggs with trimmings. When dry, put a little surprise in each and hide them for a hunt or put in Easter baskets.

FINGER-JELLO EGGS

Supplies needed:
- finger Jello liquid (see recipe in chap. 9)
- 12 raw eggs and egg carton
- funnel
- needle

Poke a tiny needle hole in the end of egg and a larger hole in top. Blow egg and gently wash it out. Place eggs in carton. With a funnel, carefully pour finger Jello into top of each egg. A little gelatin will seep out of bottom needle hole, but it will seal itself. Place in refrigerator. When gelatin is solid, your child can peel the shell off and eat the see-through egg! You can also dye the eggs before blowing. Place in Easter baskets too!

LUNCH SACK EASTER BASKET

Supplies needed:
    small, white lunch sack
    scissors
    glue
    cotton ball
    black felt marker
Cut out a rabbit ear on each of the narrow sides of bag. Draw bunny face on one wide side and glue cotton ball tail on opposite side. Staple small strip of paper to join ear tips for a handle.

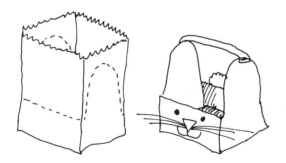

WALLPAPER EGGS

Supplies needed:
    wallpaper
    paint
    brushes
    scissors
Cut wallpaper into large egg shapes. Paint on top of printed design for interesting decorations. If you are able to find flocked wallpaper, color the flocking with wet chalk for still another experience.

GOOP EGGS

Supplies needed:
    paper
    scissors
    goop in squeeze bottles
Cut out egg shapes from paper and decorate with goop (see chap. 9 for goop recipe.)

There are many ways to decorate eggs. Here are just a few:

RUBBER CEMENT EGGS

Supplies needed:
    rubber cement
    small paint brush
    hard-boiled eggs
    egg dye and containers for dye
Paint designs on eggs with rubber cement. When dry, dip in egg dye. After dye is dry, rub off cement and either leave white or dip in another color.

TISSUE PAPER EGGS

Supplies needed:
    colored tissue paper
    liquid starch
    hard-boiled eggs
    paint brush
Brush starch on eggs and lay colored tissue on top. Overlay the colors. When completely covered, finish by brushing starch all over eggs.

RICK-RACK EGGS

Supplies needed:
    hard-boiled eggs
    rick-rack, sequins, ribbon, etc.
    glue
Glue trimmings onto egg. Give to someone special or use in an egg hunt.

NATURAL EGG DYES

Supplies needed:
    1 T. vinegar
    glass or enamel pot with lid
    water
    container for storing overnight
    carrot skins, carrot tops, spinach,
        walnuts, rhubarb, yellow onion
        skins, blackberries, red cabbage, or
        beet skins
In pot of water, put eggs and vinegar. Cover eggs with skins and replace lid on pot. Boil about one half hour. Put eggs and skins in container overnight in refrigerator. In the morning, you'll find eggs have changed col-

or! What color do you think beet skins will make? Walnuts? Guess before beginning this activity, then see if you're right!

Supplies needed:
    crayons
    hard-boiled eggs
    egg dye
    containers for dye
Crayon designs on egg, then dip into dye.

WATERCOLOR EGGS

Supplies needed:
    watercolors
    paint brush
    hard-boiled eggs
    container for water
Simply paint eggs with watercolors as you would paint on paper.

HALLOWEEN

Halloween can be fun *and* centered away from the spirit world by accentuating pumpkins:

PUMPKIN NECKLACES

Supplies needed:
    air-dry play dough (see recipe in
       chap. 9)
    paint
    paper clip
    yarn
    pumpkin cookie cutter or circle-shaped
       cutter
After clay is made, use cookie cutter to make pumpkin cut-outs. Slip paper clip into back of each pumpkin (for a hook). Let dry and paint. String yarn through clip and wear.

PAPER BAG PUMPKIN

Supplies needed:
    brown lunch or grocery bag
    orange and black paint
    brushes
    string
    newspaper

Stuff bag with newspaper until bursting. Tie with string. Paint pumpkin and decorate face with construction paper or black paint. Hang or put in a place of honor on your table.

CAN YOU DO IT?

Supplies needed:
    orange construction paper
    glue
    Cheerios, yarn, popcorn, etc.
Draw a pumpkin on paper and put glue around the pumpkin's shape. Decorate by placing Cheerios, yarn, or popcorn on glue.

PUMPKIN PLACEMAT

Supplies needed:
    orange and black paper
    glue
    scissors
    contact paper (optional)
Draw a pumpkin on orange paper and decorate by gluing eyes, nose, and mouth on it with black paper. To preserve it, cover with clear contact paper.

STUFFED PUMPKIN

Supplies needed:
    butcher paper
    stapler
    string or yarn
    newpaper
Cut out two circles for the two sides of a pumpkin. Paint a face on each piece. Staple the two sides together until there is just a small opening in the top. Stuff with newspaper, finish stapling, and hang.

OTHER THINGS TO DO WITH PUMPKINS!

Plant pumpkin seeds in the ground or in a container.
Make a book about what the seed needs in order to grow (about four pages).
Place seeds on a cookie sheet, sprinkle with vegetable oil, and roast at 350 degrees for 30 minutes . . . yum!
Make pumpkin pie, pumpkin bread, or pumpkin cookies together.

Be sure to carve a pumpkin together!

Visit a pumpkin patch to find just the right pumpkin (and how about one for a friend who may not be able to afford one, or who is sick?).

Talk about how God gives us pumpkins and all their uses.

Serve a stew dinner in a hollowed-out pumpkin.

Turn out all the lights and watch your pumpkin glow, while singing made-up pumpkin songs. Thank God for sunshine, light bulbs, candles, and flashlights so that we can see.

Have a pumpkin party! (See "Pumpkin Day" in chap. 23.)

THANKSGIVING

HAND-PRINT TURKEYS

Supplies needed:
    paint
    paper
    shallow tray for paint

Place hand in paint with fingers spread apart. Print onto paper. Make a whole turkey farm! Add beaks, legs, grass, and so on, when turkeys are dry.

LEAF TURKEY

Supplies needed:
    leaves
    paper
    glue

Draw outline of a turkey on paper. Gather leaves for its tail. Put glue on tail area, and arrange leaves on top of glue.

A THANKFUL TREE

Supplies needed:
    paper
    scissors
    tape
    pen

Trace around the hand of each member of your family and let them cut out the hands, if able. Make a tree trunk and tape to refrigerator. Write on each person's hand what he is thankful for. Tape hands onto tree to look like leaves.

OTHER THINGS TO DO AT THANKSGIVING

-Make cornbread or popcorn.

-Talk about all that God has given us—how He shares all that He has with us.

-Have unusual gourds on the table for looking and touching.

-Let your child help in the preparation of the Thanksgiving dinner (things that can be made ahead).

-Invite someone to Thanksgiving dinner who may not have a place to go.

-Take a dinner to someone who is housebound.

-Make a friend an "I'm thankful for you" card.

-Have a Thanksgiving feast (see chap. 23).

CHRISTMAS

Make use of Christmas colors and paint with red and green paint. Make red or green play dough (see recipe in chap. 9).

HAND-PRINT WREATHS

Supplies needed:
    paper
    green or red paint
    yarn or ribbon
    glue

Draw a circle on white paper. Your child puts his hand in green paint and prints all around the circle. Then he dots red berries in and out of the handprint holly with his finger. Add yarn or ribbon bow. A wonderful yearly reminder of how your child is growing!

SHAPE WREATH

Supplies needed:
    green paper

52

different colored paper shapes of
varying sizes
glue
Cut wreath out of green paper and decorate with colored paper shapes. Add a bow and hang.

Supplies needed:
paper plate or construction paper
glue
yarn or ribbon
anything to decorate with
Cut middle out of paper plate, or make a wreath shape out of paper. Glue on anything to decorate, such as styrofoam squiggles, old jewelry, aluminum foil pieces, macaroni, beans, buttons, popcorn. Add a yarn or ribbon bow and hang.

Here are some simple ornaments to make that are fun for little hands:

YARN WREATH ORNAMENT

Supplies needed:
small pieces of cardboard
light green yarn
dark green yarn
scissors
Cut out cardboard into wreath shapes. Tie dark green yarn to the circle and wrap it around and around the cardboard until all of the paper is covered. Then tie light green yarn onto circle and do the same, allow ing dark green yarn underneath to show through. Hang with yarn on your tree. A candy cane shape using red and white yarn is fun, too.

WOODEN LOOP ORNAMENT

Supplies needed:
small wooden loop or circle (from a
hobby shop or fabric store)
glue
photo of child or family member
scissors
Put glue around edge of one side of loop. Lay the photo on top. Let dry. Cut off excess photo and hang with yarn.

POPSICLE STICK ORNAMENT

Supplies needed:
three Popsicle sticks
glue
paint
glitter
piece of yarn
brush
Glue Popsicle sticks together at their centers so they look like a six-pointed star. Paint ornament when dry, add glitter, and hang with piece of yarn glued to one of the points.

EGG CARTON ORNAMENT

Supplies needed:
egg carton (cardboard type)
piece of yarn
paint
brush
glitter
Cut out individual cups from egg carton. Poke a hole in the bottom of each cup, and attach pieces of yarn to each. Now you have bells! Paint and glitter them or use permanent markers.

MEAT TRAY ORNAMENT

Supplies needed:
styrofoam meat tray
paper napkin with picture on it
liquid starch
diluted glue
brushes
piece of yarn
scissors
Brush diluted glue onto one side of styrofoam tray. Lay illustration from napkin on top of glue. Put layer of starch on top. When dry, poke hole in top of tray, and hang with yarn. The side of the tray can be decorated in same way. You can also glue old Christmas cards on meat tray and eliminate the starch.

COOKIE CUTTER ORNAMENT

Supplies needed:
air-dry dough or baker's clay
(see chap. 9 for recipes)

cookie cutters
paint
brushes
glitter or sequins
piece of yarn

After making play dough, cut out patterns with cookie cutter. Allow to air dry. Paint and add glitter or sequins. Hang with yarn. (Be sure to poke a hole in the dough for hanging before dough dries.)

CHRISTMAS CARD TREE

Supplies needed:
large piece of green paper
glue
old Christmas cards
scissors

Cut out a Christmas tree outline using green paper. Cut up old Christmas cards and glue them all over tree. Hang on your door.

SAND TREE

Supplies needed:
green paper
glue bottle
sand

Cut out tree outline from green paper. Just as in sand painting, decorate tree by squirting patterns over tree with glue bottle. Cover tree with sand. When sand is shaken off, tree is decorated. Colored sand can be made by mixing powered tempera paint and sand. Store in a shaker container.

See also the "Reindeer Antlers" hat in chapter 6.

OTHER SPECIAL THINGS TO DO FOR CHRISTMAS

-String popcorn.

-String cranberries.

-Paint and decorate Christmas cookies (see recipe for cookie paint in chap. 19, "Cooking").

-Have a piñata as the Mexican children do.

-Look into the Christmas traditions of other lands and try them.

-Use an Advent calendar to count down the days to Jesus' birthday.

-Have a special activity calendar for the month. As a door is opened each day, there is a special activity that the family or child gets to do.

-Put out a nativity scene—one that your child can handle without breaking. If you don't have one, use your child's dolls or make paper people with butcher paper stuffed with newspaper. Just draw or paint on the features.

-Encourage your little ones to think of Christmas as a time for sharing and giving by giving special food baskets you've both prepared for a needy individual or families. You can also encourage them to give one of their old, unbroken toys to a needy child or to an organization that deals with the poor, such as Toys for Tots.

-Put peanut butter on a pine cone and roll in birdseed for a bird feeder. This is one way to show how we can share even with animals.

-Get a large soup bone from the grocery store as a present to your dog.

-During this busy season, children can feel rushed and actually neglected as we shop and decorate. Let your child be part of the decorating and cooking, and, most of all, give him lots of hugs and kisses and tell him how much you love him!

-Tape record any meaningful family events during the season for later listening.

-Act out the Christmas story, with members of the family as the actors. Use a doll for baby Jesus and as few props as possible. Invite Grandma and Grandpa or a neighbor to watch.

-Visit a live manger scene in your town.

-Paint windows with snow or Christmas scenes (see glass window paint recipe in chap. 9).

You and your children can bake and decorate a cake for Jesus. Put up a few streamers and balloons and invite a few friends. Sing "Happy Birthday" to Jesus and be sure to pray, "Thank You, Jesus, for coming," before digging in!

Other activities at the party might be:

-Read a simple version of the Christmas story.

-Have an unbreakable manger scene available for handling. If it's small enough it can be used as a table centerpiece.

-If children are old enough, they can act out the story with a few props.

-Have a piñata as the Mexican children use at their birthday parties.

-Play regular games with a Christmas theme, such as "Pin the Star on the Tree" or "Hot Present" ("Hot Potato").

-Paint and decorate prebaked Christmas cookies (see recipe for cookie paint in chap. 19).

9

Special
Art Recipes*

AIR-DRY CLAY

3 c. flour
1 c. salt
½ c. glue
1 c. water
1 tsp. lemon juice
Cut with cookie cutters or mold into shapes. Let dry overnight and paint.

MY FAVORITE COOKED PLAY DOUGH RECIPE

(When kept in a plastic bag or sealed storage bag in refrigerator, it keeps forever!)
3 c. flour
1½ c. salt
6 T. vegetable oil
3 tsp. cream of tartar
3 c. water (add food coloring to water first)
A few drops of food coloring
Mix all dry ingredients, then add oil and water (with food coloring already mixed in water). Put in a pot on low heat and stir constantly. As the dough cooks, it will lump up until it becomes one large lump. It is ready when it's not sticky. Let cool completely, and keep turning it as it cools to prevent stickiness on underside. Store in refrigerator.

UNCOOKED PLAY DOUGH

3 c. flour
1 c. salt
1 c. water (with food coloring already added)

*Many thanks for the art recipes to Dr. Joyce Huggins of the Early Childhood Department at California State University, Fresno.

½ c. oil
Mix dry ingredients, then add oil and water. Mix well and store in a sealed plastic bag. Do not refrigerate.

SAWDUST DOUGH

2 parts sawdust
1 part wheat paste
water
Add wheat paste to enough water to make a smooth consistency. Add sawdust until pliable and dough-like. Mold and shape. Let dry at room temperature for several days.

PEANUT BUTTER PLAY DOUGH

It's edible!
1 c. creamy peanut butter
1 c. corn syrup
1¼ c. non-fat dry milk
1¼ c. powdered sugar
Mix until it becomes like dough. Eat while you play!

BAKER'S CLAY

4 c. flour
1 c. salt
1½ c. water
Mix all ingredients with hands (more water may be needed). Knead for five minutes, and it's ready to use. Mold with hands or use cookie cutters.

COFFEE-GROUNDS DOUGH

2 c. coffee grounds
1½ c. cornmeal

½ c. salt
water
Mix dry ingredients together and add water to make a dough consistency.

FINGER PAINT

1 T. liquid starch
1 T. liquid paint (powdered is fine)
Dishwashing liquid—a few drops (this will help paint mixture wash off hands easily)
Mix all ingredients together and paint.

PUDDING FINGER PAINT

1 package of instant pudding
2 c. milk
Beat according to directions and have fun!

GOOP

Add equal parts of:
flour
salt
water
Mix all ingredients well and put into squeeze bottles. Add food coloring or a blob of paint to each bottle. Shake well until completely mixed.

GLASS WINDOW PAINT

1 c. Bon Ami
1 c. glass paint or whitening (available at hardware or paint stores)
1 c. dry tempera paint
water
Mix all ingredients together, with enough water to make a paste consistency. Paint on with brush. It will wash off easily.

SOAP BUBBLES

½ inch of water in a pie pan
several big squirts of dishwashing liquid
Mix *gently.* See chapter 13, "Outdoor Play," for uses.

CORNSTARCH GOO

See chapter 7 for recipe.

SPECIAL CRAYONS

old broken crayons
greased muffin tins
Take broken crayons and place in well-greased muffin tins. Put in 400-degree oven until melted. Let cool before removing new crayons from tin. You can also mix the colors together for unusual crayons.

FINGER JELLO

2½ packages unflavored gelatin
1 c. cold water
Mix and set 15 minutes.
1 6-oz. box flavored gelatin
1¼ c. water
½ c. sugar
Mix and bring to a boil.
Combine both mixtures and add one cup cold water. Pour into 8"x8" pan greased or sprayed with vegetable oil. Chill until set. Remove from pan, and child can cut it up with a blunt knife, cookie cutters, etc. When done, melt down and refrigerate again. Harmless if eaten.

A TIME TO DISCOVER

10
Science

Go for a walk together around your yard. Look for blossoms on flowers or trees. Note the changes due to whatever season you're in. Talk about how wind and bird droppings help spread seeds. Feel tree trunks, noting how they need bark for protection from weather and tiny insects. Hug a tree! Make a nature collage (see chap. 5). Make a leaf finger puppet (see chap. 16 for possible ideas).

BIRD FEEDER

Make a bird feeder by spreading peanut butter on a pine cone and then rolling it in birdseed or bread crumbs. Hang with yarn or string in the yard.

NATURE CRAWL

Crawl along the grass and dirt and see what you notice or find. Use a magnifying glass for added fun and interest.

SPRING

Plant bulbs and spread flower seeds together. Then as they grow, notice each stage the plants are in. Plant the seeds so that when they sprout, they spell your child's name or make a shape.

VEGETABLE GARDEN

Maybe your child would like to plant a vegetable garden of her very own. She can help keep it watered and weeded too. What a thrill to harvest her own vegetables. And she will probably eat them—with relish!

GROWING SEEDS

There are numerous ways to grow seeds other than in your yard:

-Spread birdseed or grass seed onto a wet sponge and put in a dark place, keeping the sponge moist, until seeds germinate. See how the root system and stem come out of the center of the seed.

-Place several lima beans around the inside of a glass, held in place with wet paper toweling. Put in a dark place, and keep paper moist until seeds have sprouted. Then plant outdoors.

-Cut the top off of a potato and throw away. Scoop out some pulp from the potato and put dirt and grass seed in the hole. Put toothpicks around the potato to steady it in a cup. Wet the top of the potato and watch "hair" grow on its head!

-Grow a plant from a sweet potato, avocado, or onion (onions grow fast). Put in a jar of water, pointed end down, and hold in place with toothpicks.

-Grow carrots, turnips, radishes, beets, and so on by cutting the tops off and placing tops in a dish of water.

-Grow alfalfa sprouts to eat! Seeds can be purchased in a health food or grocery store. Put 1 to 2 tablespoons in a jar and soak overnight. Put cheesecloth over mouth of jar and secure with rubber band. Drain. Place in cupboard and rinse twice daily. In four or five days the jar will be full. Then place in direct sunlight to green up the leaves. Use in sandwiches, salads, or just for munching!

-Plant any kind of seeds in a pie pan filled with good soil. Plant the seeds so that as they grow they spell your child's name.

-Have a puppet plant an imaginary seed or make a flower glove puppet or rod puppet (see chap. 16 for ideas).

-For spring, grow tulip bulbs outdoors in a pot.

-For winter, grow narcissus bulbs outdoors in a pot.

FEED THE DUCKS

Go to a local park where there are ducks, and feed them old bread scraps. Talk about ducks needing food to eat in order to grow. What else do they need? Why don't ducks get wet in the water? Why do they need webbed feet?

CATERPILLARS TO BUTTERFLIES

Nature kits can be purchased for watching caterpillars turn into butterflies. There are also kits for ant farms, silkworms, and hermit crabs (see Resources). Make a nature cup puppet of caterpillar and butterfly (see chap. 16). Make paper butterfly wings, and tie to shoulders.

MEAT-EATING PLANTS

Buy a Venus's flytrap or pitcher plant (purchased at nurseries, or see Resources for ordering that nature kit). Plant in a terrarium-style setting. Feed the plant tiny bits of hamburger or flies about twice a month.

AQUARIUM

How about the two of you setting up an aquarium or a simple fish bowl? Talk about what fish need to live, which includes dutiful cleaning of the bowl. Goldfish are best for little ones since they're so hardy. Make Wilbur Whale to eat (see chap. 19). Act out being a fish in an aquarium.

POLLIWOGS TO FROGS

Polliwogs from a nearby pond are fun to watch develop and then let go. Make polliwog and frog puppets (see chap. 16 for ideas). Make finger puppets of each stage of a frog's life.

ANIMAL FOOTPRINTS

Look for animal footprints in dirt, dried mud, and even on cars. How many can you find? To what animal does each belong? Make your own footprints with paint (see "Footsie Hanging" in chap. 4), or make your own mud and wade in it! Check out a public library book on animal tracks.

ICE CUBES

Along the edges and in the middle of a large block of ice, put several drops of red, blue, and yellow food coloring. As the ice melts, the colors drip and blend together, making new colors.

WATER TO ICE

Make ice cubes or Popsicles, and watch the water harden at each stage. Put ice cubes on a hot sidewalk, and watch them melt. Then go run in the sprinkler!

SINK AND FLOAT

Gather objects that are heavier and lighter than water. Using a tub of water, find out which will sink and which will float. Put the objects that are heavier than water in one pile and those lighter than water in another. Can you find *more* things to float?

MAGNIFYING GLASS

Children love to experiment with a magnifying glass. Get them used to using it correctly, and then let them examine objects indoors and out.

MAGNETS

What will a magnet stick to? Gather objects that have steel or lead in them, and some that don't (plastic, wood, glass, paper). Those drawn to the magnet put in one pile; those that are repelled in another. Can you find *more* objects around the house and outdoors to try?

THE SENSE OF SMELL

Using empty film containers or other plastic containers with lids, fill with various substances such as cinnamon, cloves, onions, lemons, and garlic. Smell them and decide which ones you like and which you don't. What do these smells remind you of? Do you know the names of the substances making the aromas? Have you smelled them before when Mom was cooking? Guess what they are, and then peek inside.

SENSE OF HEARING

Using plastic containers, film canisters, or plastic eggs, fill each with different sounding objects (beans, macaroni, bottle caps, rocks, sand, paper clips). Shake them. Which is the quietest? Loudest? In between? Can you arrange them from quietest to loudest? What do you think is inside the containers? Guess, then peek!

SENSE OF TASTE

Cut up small pieces of lemon, apple, pineapple, onion, as well as a ¼ teaspoon each of sugar, cinnamon, flour, and brown sugar. Close your eyes and smell each first. Then taste them. Which are sweet? Sour? Bitter? Which do you like? Don't like? Guess what they are before opening your eyes.

SENSE OF TOUCH

Have your child close his eyes, and lead him around touching and feeling objects and guessing what they are. Do they feel soft? Rough? Scratchy? Smooth? Bumpy? You can also make a "feel box" by cutting a hole in a shoe box lid and filling the box with varied objects. Replace the lid, and let your child put his hand in the hole and describe the object. How does it feel? What do you think it is? Then pull it out to look at it.

WATCH ME GROW

Keep a measuring chart of your child's growth. Point out how much he has grown in a certain amount of time. Talk about what his body needs to grow: food (milk, meat, bread, fruits, and vegetables), exercise, and water. Paint a picture of yourself (see "Paint Yourself" in chap. 4). Make a Funny Foot Puppet (see chap. 16). Make a photo time line: with a long strip of paper, tape photos representing your child at infancy through to the present. Put the earliest pictures at the bottom of the time line and the most recent at the top.

NIGHT SIGHT

Go out and spend time gazing at the moon and stars. What do you think they look like close up? What other lights do you see? Airplanes? Shooting stars? Listen to the noises at night. What do you hear? Why do we need night? Make a star finger puppet. Dab white paint (stars) onto black paper (sky). Add glitter, too.

BONES

Feel your elbows, knees, ribs, skull, and talk about bones. Can you find any more? What would you be like without bones? How do they help us? Make a skeleton from spaghetti, maraconi, or pretzel sticks. Lie down on a piece of paper, and outline your body. Paint or draw in bones. Make a skeleton Body-Bag Puppet (see chap. 16).

PETS

Besides the usual dog or cat, you can buy hermit crabs, fish, hamsters, lizards, rabbits, birds, mice, and guinea pigs. Special instructions in handling and care are essential and easy to explain if you use a dog puppet, for example, to explain how he likes to be cared for. Visit a pet shop.

DINOSAURS

Little children have a fascination with dinosaurs. Read lots of dinosaur books. Make your footprint in mud, then make a dinosaur footprint! Make Alvin Allosaurus (see chap. 19), or make a dinosaur puppet (see Pot Holder Puppets). Make a dinosaur out of play dough and use toothpicks for spines along its back and tail. Make a papier-maché terrain on a rectangular piece of wood. Buy small plastic dinosaurs to roam on it or use the play dough dinosaurs.

RAINBOWS

During early morning or late afternoon, spray a garden hose away from the sun to make a rainbow! What colors do you see? Which colors are on the top half? Bottom half? Can you paint a rainbow? Make a rainbow puppet (see "Dancing Rainbows" in chap. 16).

INSECTS

Look for insects under rocks. Then make an edible insect (see chap. 19). Listen and look for bees. Make a honey and peanut butter sandwich. Make an insect puppet. Sing a song about bees or make up a song about bugs using rhythm instruments. Make an antennae headband (see chap. 6). Collect bugs in a see-through container to observe and let go. Make an insect from baker's clay and glue onto a broach pin (see recipe in chap. 9).

VISIT TIDE POOLS

What do you see as you climb among the tide pools at the beach? Collect shells and different types of seaweed, moss, and driftwood.

Look at all the different things God has made! What good is the sea? (Food, recreation, transportation). What foods come from the ocean? Make a collage with your new-found treasures. Make a sand painting (see chap. 4).

WEATHER CHART

Make a circle from stiff paper and divide it into sections by drawing three intersecting lines. Draw pictures in each pie section representing foggy, sunny, rainy, snowy, windy, and stormy weather. Make a paper arrow and attach to the middle of the circle with a brad. It's great fun each morning to discover what the weather is like and to point the arrow to the correct picture. Talk about what rain is good for. What happens after it rains? Why do we need the wind? Cut a strip of crepe paper, and run in the wind! Buy a pinwheel and run with it. (I have found that store-bought pinwheels work better and last longer than home-made ones.)

HABITATS

Visit any museum of natural history in your area, tide pools, zoo, pet shops, or aquarium stores to reinforce the understanding of specific animals and their habitats (including what they eat, when they sleep, and how their particular habitats are best for them).

MAGAZINES

There are wonderful nature magazines for little ones available by subscription (see Resources). These have large, colorful photos of animals with simple explanations. They also have stories and activity pages.

SHADOWS

Why do we have shadows? Could we have shadows without light? How many can you find during the day? At night? Put your hands between a lamp and a wall. Make shapes with your hands and body. Draw your child's head silhouette onto paper. Let her draw yours! Paint a black and white "shadow" picture. Make a shadow puppet (see chap. 16).

11
Concepts

God made your child such that, as he progresses developmentally, he will become increasingly interested in abstract concepts. You will have great enjoyment together with numbers and letters, sorting and patterning. But it's important to remember not to rush that interest. The time to begin is when *he* is ready— when he is truly interested.

Here are some ideas I call "natural," because most of the concepts can be drawn from your environment naturally. These are not concepts to sit down and teach. Any skills acquired will be a by-product of your quality time together.

SORTING

Sort according to shape, kind, color, size:

-Sort big dolls and little dolls, big trucks and little trucks.

-Sort plastic flowers according to colors and kind.

-Sort buttons, beads, different types of macaroni, seeds. Use a muffin tin.

-Sort alphabet noodles, and then make alphabet soup together!

-Sort magazine pictures of people, animals, cars, happy and sad faces.

-Sort farm and zoo animals or animals that live on land, in sea, and in air.

-Sort plastic knives, forks, and spoons.

-Sort big, medium, and small books.

PATTERNING

The child reproduces the identical pattern:

-Using macaroni, seeds, colored toothpicks, blocks, beads, place a sequence or pattern on the floor, and see if your child can duplicate it. Then let him make a pattern for you to duplicate.

-Clapping. Clap out a simple two- or three-pattern clap and have child imitate.

-Pegboard. Set up a sequence of colored pegs to be reproduced.

-Make a pattern of books according to size (big, small, medium, small, medium).

COLORS

-Wear a certain color all day or all week.

-Take a colored bath using food coloring!

-Make orange juice Popsicles or other flavor.

-Bake cookies and decorate with colored frosting.

-Play with colored play dough (see recipe in chap. 9).

-Draw attention to flowers, blossoms, fruits, when outdoors.

-Have a color party: decorate cookies, make blue lemonade (food coloring in lemonade), and paint pictures!

-Make colored lemonade: put food coloring in ice cubes and freeze. Place cubes in lemonade and watch it turn color as cubes melt.

-Blow colored bubbles (see "Outdoor Play").

-Use any of the painting ideas in chapter 4.

-Make a rainbow puppet (see chap. 16)

SHAPES

-Make cookies using different shaped cookie cutters.

-Notice shapes in things around the house: the pizza is a circle, the windows are rectangular, the pillow is a triangle.

-Cut out bread, toast, Jello in various shapes.

-Do artwork on different shaped paper.

-Contrast blocks as to shapes and size.

-Make shapes with play dough.

-Make shapes in air with your fingers.

-Glue colored, shaped papers onto large paper. See what animals you can make from circles, triangles, squares, and rectangles.

AWARENESS OF NUMBERS

-Set the table. How many plates do we need? Forks? Spoons? Napkins?

-Make an Advent calendar at Christmas time to count down the days.

-Make a birthday advent calendar to use a week before that special day! The bright stickers now available are perfect for counting down.

-Pick up toys. Count how many cars or how many toys picked up in all.

-Draw attention to specific dates on calendar: date to go to Grandma's, birthdays, trip to zoo.

-Use terms such as *more, less, dozen, half*.

-Weigh yourself and your child at home—keep a chart.

-Weigh vegetables and fruit at grocery store.

-Measure with yardstick, ruler, and tape measure.

-Keep a growth chart on your child where he can see it.

-Measure, count, and so on, when cooking.

-While driving, count houses with chimneys, blue trucks, etc.

-Read books such as *The Three Little Pigs* or *Snow White and the Seven Dwarfs*.

-Mention specific times that you do things, such as naptime is at 1:00, lunchtime is at 12:00, time for favorite TV show is 4:00, bedtime is 8:00.

-Number cookie cutters are fun and are available at specialty stores.

-Count when grocery shopping: five oranges, two boxes of cereal, etc.

-Estimate how many cookies are in the box or candies in the bag.

-Use fingerplays that incorporate numbers (see Resources).

-Experiment with filling different containers with sand or water (estimating).

-Periodically check indoor and outdoor thermometers.

-Play store with toy money.

-Let your child help pay for things at the checkout counter.

-Let him have coins for his piggy bank and to spend at a later time.

-Play with an old phone or help dial a real one.

-Put magnetic numbers on refrigerator to play with.

AWARENESS OF LETTERS

-Sing ABC songs.

-Notice letter shapes in familiar objects such as a pipe resembling the letter *L* or a garden hose like the letter *S*.

-Read, read, read to your child! And be sure he sees you reading by yourself!

-Make letters with play dough.

-Make letters with play dough, and let them air dry. Paint them and wear as a necklace (see "Heart Necklaces" in chap. 8 for procedure).

-Draw attention to billboards, signs, grocery bags.

-Any sorting game aids awareness because it helps the child perceive differences in shapes, which is needed in order to begin reading.

-Paint a shoe box black inside, and, when dry, cover bottom with a small layer of salt (or sand). Your child can then draw letters he sees in the salt. The black bottom of the box shows through.

-Have magnetic letters on the refrigerator to play with.

-Sort alphabet noodles or alphabet cereal.

-Cook a specific letter each week: Hairy Harvey for the letter *H* (see chap. 19 for ideas).

-Write your child's name on things, and spell it out loud as you write.

-Write letters in the sand or with water (see "Water Painting," chap. 4).

-While traveling: "I see something that starts with the letter *M,* the Mmmmm sound."

-Read alphabet books.

-Plant seeds in the ground or in a planter in the shape of specific letters—or to spell your child's name.

TIME

-Mention specific times to do things.

-Discuss events that precede and follow other events.

-Use terms such as *before, after, the day before.*

-Discuss why some things take longer to do than others.

-Put a travel clock in bedroom for play and observation.

LISTENING

-Go outdoors and listen. Name all the different sounds and their sources. Do the same with indoor sounds.

-Hide a kitchen timer that ticks audibly. Can you find the timer in the living room? When child does, let her hide it from you!

-Read, read, read stories to your child every day!

-Enjoy clapping (same as used in "Patterning").

-Use taped stories where child must turn page at the signal.

-Hap Palmer records are terrific for listening and doing (see Resources).

-Attend story time at the library.

-Play a listening game: Begin with two directions. Child follows them in order. Stamp your feet and clap your hands, or touch your nose and turn around. Graduate to three directions when two become too easy.

RHYMING

-Read nursery rhymes, and encourage your child to learn them with you.

-Start a rhyme, and have child finish it with the correct rhyming word ("Little Miss Muffet sat on a . . .").

-Tell child that you are thinking of an animal on the farm that rhymes with "fig."

-Listen to songs and find the rhyming words in them.

-Look through magazines and find two objects that rhyme.

For further reinforcement of all the above concepts, try *Sesame Street Magazine.* It's a wonderful, enjoyable, colorful, and thorough magazine that preschool children love (see Resources).

A TIME TO PLAY

12
Manipulative Toys

Manipulative toys are fun to do together. They are mind-stretching too, because they allow a child to discover for himself their many uses. A good manipulative toy can be used in more than one or two ways. There are excellent ones on the market. Here are a few ideas to get you started.

Puzzles. Be sure to start with only three- or four-piece puzzles and work up to more pieces.

Sand play. See chapter 13, "Outdoor Play."

Water play. See chapter 13.

Building Toys. Legos, Bristle Blocks, Lincoln Logs, Waffle Blocks, and Tinker Toys are all excellent for older preschoolers.

Blocks. If you can afford to get two different sizes of blocks, that's great. When setting them out, add trucks, signs, trees, people, and so on, to enhance the play.

Homemade blocks. Cut tops off of two cardboard milk cartons and insert one open end into the other. Press together and cover with plastic contact paper to seal and decorate.

Stringing beads. Available in most toy and educational supply stores.

Stringing junk. String plastic lids, toilet tissue tubes, spools, paper plates, or aluminum pie plates onto stiff shoelace or plastic tubing. You can also string cut plastic straws, Cheerios, and macaroni.

Puppets. See chapter 16 for homemade ideas.

Pegboard. Available in most toy and educational supply stores.

Geo-boards. Hammer nine to twelve nails into a small square pine board (about 12″ x 12″). Allow half of each nail to show. Using colored rubber bands make shapes and designs by wrapping the bands around the nails:

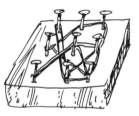

Homemade town. Get a large piece of green quilted material (the stiffer the better). Sew on roads, train tracks, pond, store outlines. Your child can use cars, train, animals, and people with it. When finished playing, fold it up!

Play dough. See recipe in chapter 9. Use rolling pin, cookie cutters, kitchen utensils with interesting surfaces with the dough.

Felt flannelboard. Cover cardboard with flannel material and, using precut shapes of houses, cars, trees, people, and animals, make up stories on the flannelboard. Plain string can also be used on flannelboard to make up shapes, stories, letters, and designs.

Sometimes your Sunday school super-intendent will let you have flannel-backed Bible figures that are no longer needed at church.

Creative play. Have available a place where your child can cut, write, draw, and color whenever he wishes. Here are a few things you could have on hand:

colored felt pens
rubber stamps
  and pad
small chalkboard
  and chalk
scissors
colored construction
  paper
old Easter seals

old envelopes
old cards
stencils
crayons
pencils and
  erasers
scratch paper
stickers

13
Outdoor Play

Here are a number of ideas to augment your play outside:

Sand play. Wet part of sand for building and molding. Sifters, pails, scoops, old spoons, tractors, small toy people and animals, and other toys are a fun addition. Wooden spoons or mallets with designs or pegs on the end are great for making patterns, as are wooden or cardboard combs:

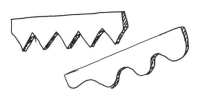

Containers with unusual shapes make interesting castle molds. Poke holes in a plastic gallon milk carton to enable sand to pour out like a sieve. A scoop can be made from a plastic gallon milk container, too:

Water play. Use an old baby bath or plastic tub. Fill with clear or colored water (food coloring). Add dishwashing liquid for different kind of fun. Employ utensils such as corks, plastic tubing, sifters, colanders, funnels, measuring cups and spoons, plastic containers (poke holes in some), a basting syringe, and a plastic doll to bathe.

Blow bubbles. Poke a hole in one end of a small orange juice can. Cut other end completely off. Using several squirts of dishwashing liquid in an aluminum pie pan, filled to ½″ mark with water, dip the open end of can in liquid, and blow through hole!

Hammering nails. You may need to get your child started by hammering the nails partway into a heavy piece of wood. Use lightweight, small-headed hammer.

Crack nuts. Use small-headed hammer to crack walnuts or other softer shelled nuts.

Tools. Use a plane, sandpaper, or even saw wood or large piece of styrofoam.

Crepe paper. Tear off a strip and run with it! It's better than a kite for young ones because it's not only easier to handle, but no windy day is needed.

Water painting. See chapter 4.

Cornmeal or macaroni play. Play with cornmeal or macaroni in plastic tub or roasting pan, using same type of utensils as in water play. (You can also make a mixture of beans, cereal, dried peas, noodles.)

Read books. It's fun to read in an unusual place. Spread a blanket on the lawn or read in a make-shift tent. Find a snuggly place to curl up and read.

Play dough. To keep dirt and sand out, use large roasting pan, piece of linoleum, or plastic tablecloth.

Boxes. Play with boxes of all sizes.

Blocks. Take outside for a change.

Balance beam. Make one using a small plank. Keep board resting on the ground until child is proficient, then raise it a few inches.

Nature walk. Take a walk and see what you can find that God has made.

Get wet. Run in the sprinkler, or sit in a plastic tub and splash.

Leaves. Gather leaves and jump in them.

Snowman. Build a snowman out of snow or tumbleweeds.

Bean bag toss. Make bean bags of any shape (such as an animal) and fill with barley or split peas or beans. Toss into a laundry basket or hula-hoop. Walk with bean bag on your head, place on foot and try to kick and catch, or toss it from one hand to the other.

Large moving or storage box. Cut out windows and door for house, or cover card table with sheet for makeshift tent.

Obstacle course. Use anything handy and create obstacles that will require crawling, jumping, rolling, running, and so on. Some suggestions are:

- Old tires—Bury halfway into ground for climbing on or crawling through. Lay on side for hopping over.
- Rope or string—Walk on rope. Make shapes to walk around. Put one foot in shape and one foot out. Jump inside shape. Run as fast as you can the length of the rope.
- Old paint cans or containers—Run, hop, jump around.
- Tricycles—At a certain point in the course, child must ride trike to a designated place.

- Jungle gyms—If you're lucky enough to have one, these speak for themselves!
- Hula-Hoops—Jump inside, run around inside and outside, jump through.

Large tires. Large truck or tractor tires can be used to climb in, or may be filled with sand for a sandbox. When half buried, standing up, they can be climbed on and through. Hang a car tire from a rope in a tree and you have a tire swing.

Croquet. There are children's indoor/outdoor croquet games available if you don't already have one for adults.

Balls. Kick ball around, toss it, roll it, bounce it.

Nancy's idea. Using a sawed-off broomstick and a large plastic soda bottle, put the sawed end of the stick into the bottle neck, and wrap the joint tightly with strong electrical tape. Now you have a fail-proof bat to hit the ball as it is rolled on the ground!

Dolls. Wash doll clothes or bathe dolls.

Dogs. Give your dog a bath!

Dishes. Use play dish set and have a tea party. When finished, wash dishes in a tub.

A TIME TO IMAGINE

14
Creative Play

Children are born with imaginations that are developed through creative play. The more you play with your child, the more idea possibilities come to mind. One of the greatest results I've found is that not only is my child's imagination stimulated, but that through sharing in creative play together, godly character qualities are developed and reinforced—such as kindness toward animals and people, sympathy for others, sharing, a desire to help others and to right wrongs. You will find most often the play situation creates the opportunity, and from there your child responds. As *you* respond, you become a role model, and positive character qualities are then shared. It's a wonderful exchange, and so much can be learned about your child.

Creative play also enhances language skills, cooperation, and problem solving and gives the child a feeling of control over his environment. A well-developed child role-plays frequently whether he pretends to be a doctor, actress, or super-hero, or talks to a rabbit that lives on the ceiling! Encourage fantasizing by playing along. Ask what the rabbit likes to eat, or tell him that a little puppy needs the help of a super-hero. Pretend you are a make-believe character. Any hats or objects around the house can enhance play. Some ideas might be:

-Set up a "scene" with a cardboard box as a boat or car. Put chairs in a row for a train. You can act out your very own story, creating as you go.

-Make super-hero capes and nurses' caps, or collect a boxful of old hats from the thrift or party supply store. October is an ideal month for collecting masks, hats, and accessories for a variety of characters.

-A large moving and storage box: cut out windows and door for a playhouse.

-Cover a card table with sheet for a quick house, boat, airplane.

-Gather old shoe boxes to store various types of clothing for role playing. Some ideas might be:

DOCTOR

plastic doctor's equipment: stethoscope, thermometer, etc.
dad's old white T-shirt for uniform
doctor and nurse paper hats
cotton swabs
bandages
chairs and magazines for office equipment
dolls for patients
small plastic containers and bottles

FIREMAN

fire hat
bell for siren (other rhythm instrument will do)
rope for hose
chair, box, or tricycle for fire engine

GROCERY STORE

play money or use small bits of paper
empty cake boxes, etc.

shallow box for cash register
empty cans (watch for sharp edges)
small grocery bags
table for checkout counter
apron for grocery clerk

IMITATING MOMMY/DADDY

small razor without blade
small hand mirror
shaving cream
comb and brush
empty powder compact with powder puff
empty lipstick tube or use Chapstick
apron or bib to protect clothing!

TRAIN

chairs or empty boxes to sit in
rhythm instruments for train sounds
paper tickets
dolls or stuffed toys for passengers
whistle

JUNGLE RIVER TRIP

couch or bed for boat
toilet tissue tube telescope
canteen for water (or thermos)
stuffed toys for wild animals

PAINTER

paint hat (sold in paint stores)
old paint brushes
old paint roller
apron

CAMPING

card table and sheet for tent
sticks for campfire
stick for fishing pole
small fry pan for cooking food
sleeping bag or blanket for bedding

RESTAURANT

table
chairs
small tablecloth
play dishes or adult plastic dishes
plastic knives, forks, spoons
real food!

MORE IDEAS

-Gather old clothes from your closet or thrift shop for dressing up.

-Make a dress-up doll on a shoe box lid. Cut out a felt body shape of a boy or girl and glue onto box lid. Make clothing for it out of scrap felt and material and rick-rack. The clothes are stored inside the box until the child wants to dress the doll.

-Storytelling flannelboard: Cut out a large felt rectangle, or cover a piece of sturdy cardboard with flannel material. Then cut out shapes from other pieces of colored felt such as houses, trees, animals, cars, space ships, sun, moon, people. Your child can create stories from these, and the cutouts can be stored in an envelope taped to the back of the flannelboard.

15
Drama

You and your child will have fun re-creating situations as well as animate and inanimate objects. Here are a few ideas to get you started:

-Let's be falling leaves. Oops!—We're falling, floating down, down, down. Here comes the wind to blow us farther and faster! Now let's be leaves blown along the ground.

-Let's be snowmen melting.

-Let's be seeds in the ground. The sun is warming us, and the rain has given us a drink. Now we're beginning to grow—bigger, bigger, taller, and taller. (Grow until you are full-grown flowers or trees.)

-Pretend we are wading through peanut butter or mud!

-What animals are slow? Fast? Can you imitate them?

-Pretend we are robots. How will our arms move? Legs? How will we sound when we talk?

-Pretend we are dinosaurs eating plants. Here comes another dinosaur who wants to eat too. How will we walk? Do you have a long neck and tail or a small head and spines on your back?

-Let's curl up into a ball. Stretch out into a long snake. Twist into a curly noodle!

-Let's pretend we're rag dolls. Shake each arm and leg, flop when we walk, fall on the floor.

-Let's be elephants, and our arms are our trunks!

-Let's move with scarves—skip, jump, gallop, hop, sway, leap, bend, and stretch. Now let's do it to music.

-Let's pretend we're magnets! We're being pulled toward the refrigerator!

-Let's pretend we're popcorn popping!

16
Puppets, Wonderful Puppets

With puppets the enjoyment is doubled; making them together and then dramatizing. All children seem to have a fascination with them. The ideas selected below vary greatly in type and degree of difficulty in construction.

Keep the project short by having cloth materials precut and everything ready at hand. For the very young child, have any steps done ahead that you know would be frustrating or would result in a lack of interest.

But for the child making a puppet, satisfaction in the finished product will often depend on her freedom to create, so, as her skills allow, let her make as much of the puppet as possible. Occasionally you might choose to make a puppet for your child. Whatever you do, she will experience joy in its use.

I would like to thank Nancy Renfro and Tamara Hunt for their willingness to share the first five ideas with us and for all of their inspiration in putting this section together.*

WHAT CAN BE DONE WITH PUPPETS?

-sing songs

-repeat nursery rhymes

-act out a familiar story

-make up new stories

*See Resources for ordering Nancy Renfro and Tamara Hunt's wonderful book *Puppetry in Early Childhood Education.*

-use as a specific story character while reading a book. Make a monster finger puppet to use when reading *Where the Wild Things Are*, by Maurice Sendak (New York: Harper & Row, 1963), or a caterpillar and a butterfly puppet to use when reading *The Very Hungry Caterpillar*, by Eric Carle (New York: Philomel Books, 1981).

-counting

-saying alphabet

-hugging!

-give to a shy child

-help children talk about fears regarding divorce, a new baby, sibling relationships, death

-give to a bedridden friend

-dance with to music

-use high/low, loud/soft voice variations

-show various emotions

-help create interest in science

-just have fun with!

MAKE-SHIFT STAGES:

Stages are not necessary and often are a hindrance with preschoolers, but as your child grows older, stages can be made from turned-over card tables, a sheet between two chairs, a sheet hung in the lower half of a doorway, and even a shoe box for finger puppets.

STRING PUPPETS

Supplies needed:
- small box or pint sized milk carton, or magazine picture
- string or heavy thread
- cardboard tube or dowel rod control
- construction paper

Thread a length of string through top of box or magazine picture and secure a knot. Attach cardboard tube or dowel to other end of string for handle. Add pleated legs and decorate with flair! A ruffle added to bottom of box makes an excellent skirt; cotton glued on surface a fuzzy sheep. Note: When cutting out magazine pictures, omit legs and arms of character and replace with pleated ones instead.

THUMBPRINT PUPPETS

Supplies needed:
- ink pad with black or colored ink
- paper
- Popsicle stick for rod control

Make copies of incomplete characters below, and let children fill in missing parts of animals such as ears, tail, and body with their thumbprints. Cut out characters and tape onto rod control. Ask children to make up their own characters by adding features to one or several thumb-prints.

BRACELET PUPPETS

Supplies needed:
- 9-inch length of ribbon
- picture or felt shape

Staple any picture (drawing, magazine, greeting card, etc.) or felt shape onto center of ribbon; tie ribbon around child's wrist. Note: Though all young children enjoy wearing these puppets, they are particulary well-suited to handicapped children with limited motor control.

DANCING RAINBOWS

Supplies needed:
- paper plate, cut in thirds
- colored construction paper
- cardboard tube or other safe handle

Tape six strips of colored construction paper, each representing a color of the rainbow, onto paper plate. Attach the rainbow plate to cardboard tube. Once the puppet is constructed, encourage the children to experiment by circling their arms in the air to mimic a rainbow arch and running with their puppets to make them "fly" across the sky. Children like to dance with these puppets by moving them in time with music.

Select gentle music to inspire graceful body movements.

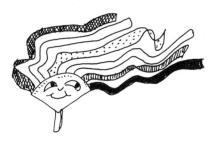

MR. FUNNY FOOT

Supplies needed:
    construction paper
    skewers or drinking straw for rod
      control

Trace around child's hand or foot onto paper and cut out. Decorate the character capitalizing on the characteristics of the hand or foot shape; attach to a rod control.

ROD PUPPETS

Supplies needed:
    straw, dowel, or tongue depressor
    glue, stapler, or tape
    magazine pictures, photos,
      greeting cards, or styrofoam ball
    construction paper or paper plate
    scissors

Here are several kinds of rod puppets to make:

1. Cut out animal, object, or person from magazine or greeting card. Glue onto construction paper. Staple picture onto tongue depressor or straw.

2. Draw a face, person, or animal on paper plate. Staple plate onto tongue depressor or dowel.

3. Press dowel onto styrofoam ball and glue in place. Decorate ball as a face. Glue on a handkerchief or fabric for body if desired. (For older preschoolers, straight pins can be used to hold handkerchief in place.)

4. Cut out photo of child, family member, or pet and glue onto tongue depressor or straw.

5. Glue construction paper shapes onto straw or tongue depressor.

6. Glue small plastic toy or stuffed animal onto dowel.

BODY-BAG PUPPET

Supplies needed:
  large grocery bag
  glue
  yarn or string
  elastic loops or rubber bands (two)
  stapler
  two strips of fabric the length of child's arm

Here is a great puppet to wear! Decorate bag with feathers, sequins, egg carton cups, yarn, or whatever, or paint on features and clothes. To wear, staple a neck strap of yarn or string to top of bag:

For arms, staple a strip of material under each side of the bag flap. Staple elastic loop or rubber band to end of each arm so that child can slip them onto wrists and wear. You can staple on cloth or paper legs too if desired.

Ideas:
  Make a beak and add feathers for a bird.

Make a favorite Bible story character and act out the story.
Make a favorite nursery rhyme or story book character.
Make an emotion—happy, angry, sad, sleepy.
Make a skeleton and draw in bones.
Add heart, stomach, lungs for added fun!

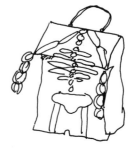

SPOON PUPPETS

Supplies needed:
  wooden or plastic spoons (large or small)
  glue
  felt pens
  felt, ribbon, cotton balls, etc., to decorate

Glue or draw features onto spoon. Add felt or paper hat, tail, etc.

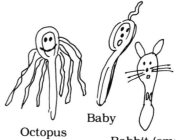

Octopus

Baby

Rabbit (small ice cream spoon)

Similar puppets can be made from household utensils.

Feather duster

Fly swatter

90

CUP PUPPETS

Supplies needed:
    styrofoam or paper cup
    drinking straws or thin dowels
    glue
    pom-poms
    construction paper
    materials for decorating

A unique way to sing songs and tell stories or invent new ones! Draw scenery around outside of cup as desired. Make a stick puppet by gluing pom-poms, magazine pictures, or photos onto straw or dowel. Poke holes in bottom of cup for stick to fit through.

Caterpillar to butterfly

Little Miss Muffet

Your family from photos backed onto thin cardboard

Ocean scene (clear plastic cup and seaweed drawn on sides of cup with felt marker)

STUFFED TOY PUPPETS

Supplies needed:
    dowel
    stuffed toy
    scissors
    needle and thread

Cut a slit behind head in the neck region and remove enough stuffing so that child's hand can easily fit inside. Move stuffing around to fill out any nose area. Overcast raw seams to prevent fraying.

SIMPLE MARIONETTES

Supplies needed:
    string or fishing line
    stick, Popsicle stick, or small piece of
        doweling
    kitchen utensils, toys, hair brush, or
        whatever

Marionettes can be made by hanging objects from string or fishing line. For easy holding, attach other end to a small piece of doweling, a stick, or a Popsicle stick.

GLOVE PUPPETS

Supplies needed:
    any glove that fits your child's hand
    glue
    pom-poms, felt, etc., for decorating
    Velcro

Wonderful glove puppets can be made with a little imagination. For the song "Jesus Loves Me" or "Jesus Loves the Little Children," glue a small Velcro strip onto each fingertip and onto each of five pom-poms (use red, yellow, brown, black, and white pom-poms for "Jesus Loves the Little Children." Jesus can be the brown pom-pom.) Add eyes, smiles, and hair to pom-pom faces using felt. Give Jesus' face a beard, and you're ready to sing the song. The Velcro allows you to use your glove interchangeably for other songs, stories, and rhymes.

Jesus Loves the Little Children

How Polliwogs Become Frogs

A black glove can be a friendly spider! Sew padding inside the back of the glove for a raised spider body. Add button or sequin eyes.

A long evening glove can be used for the story "Jack and the Beanstalk."

FINGER PUPPETS

Supplies needed:
    felt, paper, or stiff fabric scraps
    glue, or a needle and thread
    more felt, cotton balls, felt pen to
        decorate
    scissors
    stiff, thin cardboard

Sew felt or stiff material into a cylinder or fingertip shape, or a glove tip can be used.

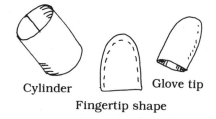

Cylinder   Glove tip
        Fingertip shape

With either shape, sew or glue the seams together and decorate.

Bat

Rabbit

Photo

Another type of finger puppet is made out of stiff paper. Cut out the desired shape and cut holes where legs or nose should be for your fingers to go in.

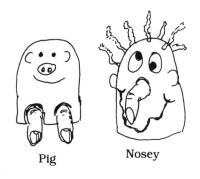

Pig   Nosey

SHADOW PUPPETS

Supplies needed:
    doweling, Popsicle stick, or drinking
        straw
    stiff paper
    masking tape
    scissors
    stapler or glue
    brad

92

Easy shadow puppets can be made by cutting out the silhouette of an animal, rocket, or person, for example. Staple silhouette to dowel. To use, place puppet between a lamp and the wall. Moving limbs can be made, too. Cut off the arm to a clown silhouette and trace around it, making another arm a little longer than the original. Make one hole in shoulder and one in top of arm. Attach with brad at shoulder. When the puppet is shaken, the arm will move. A dowel can also be taped to wrist for guided movement.

Car
(Colored tissue paper can be taped to car windows for added effect)

Clown
(Cut out features for added interest)

COIN PURSE PUPPET

Supplies needed:
    plastic coin purse
    glue
    permanent felt marker
    yarn
    construction paper or felt
    scissors
Decorate a coin purse with paper eyes and hat or yarn hair. Squeeze both sides of the purse to make puppet's mouth move.

POT HOLDER PUPPETS

Supplies needed:
    glove pot holder (or sew a quick one out
        of scraps)
    felt, yarn, etc., for decoration
    glue
    Velcro
    scissors

Here are two kinds of story pot holder puppets. For the first, make a story scene such as the ocean. Cut out felt seaweed and glue onto pot holder. Glue small strips of Velcro where fish will go. Cut out felt fish, sea horses, starfish, and glue Velcro strips onto them also. As you tell the story, put the fish onto the Velcro strips on the glove.

The second type of story pot holder is made by turning the pot holder sideways. Take a familiar story such as "The Gingerbread Man" and cut out the characters. (You can cut out paper characters right from the book, too.) Attach Velcro strips to the characters and on the pot holder where they will be.

Put one Velcro circle on the end of the glove by the fingers for the fox. When the fox gobbles up the gingerbread man, you can close your fist to make them all disappear! Another type of glove pot holder puppet is using the shape of the pot holder to design a puppet.

Girl

Dinosaur

Pumpkin

For the last type, simply add ears, nose, eyes, and a tongue for a dog, crocodile, or dragon.

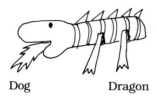

Dog   Dragon

POP-UP PUPPETS

Supplies needed:
   glue
   small oatmeal tub or juice can
   styrofoam ball
   thin doweling or drinking straw
   felt, yarn, trimmings for decoration
Glue styrofoam ball onto dowel. Add facial features, hair, ears, etc., with felt and trimmings. (Felt can also be pinned with straight pins if your child is old enough to be careful with them.) Make a hole in one end of can for dowel to fit into and have other end completely open. Place dowel inside can and out through small hole. Push up dowel to make the head pop out of the can. Decorate the can if you wish. If you'd like to give the puppet a "body," glue material from the inside edge of the can and attach at the puppet's neck with a rubber band or yarn. This also prevents the dowel from coming completely out of the can.

Mouse   Rabbit

A TIME TO SPEAK

17
Language Development

A child gains language through hearing it spoken. Whether your child has a good grasp of the language yet or not, he still needs to hear affirming talk—"I love you." "I think you're terrific!" "I like to spend time with you." "What a good idea!" "You're so strong!"

Let him hear your affirmations as often as possible. The more you affirm, the stronger his self-esteem will be and—surprise!—he'll learn affirming language as well. You'll find him using it on you—and others.

Below are a few ideas to enhance language without being forced or unnatural:

-If you use baby talk, slur, or mumble, your child will imitate what he hears.

-Don't let him point, grunt, or have older siblings talk for him if you know he can speak for himself.

-Notice what he is immediately interested in and talk about that.

-Talk about what you're doing as he helps you cook, clean, or tend to the garden.

-Use words interchangeably. If she says, "I sad," you can reply, "I'm sorry that you're unhappy."

-Don't hesitate to use words he doesn't understand yet. Often the context in which a word is used makes the word understandable.

-Nursery rhymes: Children love the sound of sing-song words, and nonsense and rhyming words delight them. Fingerplays are fun, too (see Resources).

-Read, read, read to your child! Reading enhances your close, loving relationship, increases vocabulary, and gives a love and appreciation for books. Later, you'll see an eagerness for reading.

-Take trips to the library to check out children's books. Let him use your card if he isn't able to have one yet. Take advantage of story times they offer.

-Name objects while driving, walking, cooking, or shopping. This will aid the understanding that objects often have more than one name—man/father, bird/robin, banana/fruit.

-Describe specific parts of objects. A bed has a mattress, frame, and headboard. A car has wheels, engine, steering wheel.

-Listen to children's music and story records.

-Use terms like *in between, in front of, upside-down, beside, before, after, inside, outside,* and comparisons such as *big, bigger, biggest.*

-Use puppets.

-Manipulative toys such as blocks, clay, crayons, geoboards encourage the use of language.

All of the activities listed in this book encourage language use.

A TIME TO SING

18
Music

Children have a natural love for and attraction to music. They will be drawn to whatever you play in your home and will soon make it known which songs are their favorites. There are many wonderful albums, tapes, and books available at record and Bible bookstores. Most children enjoy a variety of styles in music. The following ideas are to help provide that variety.

-Play as many kinds of music as you can from classical to jazz, and play them often. Try not to let your personal dislike for a certain type of music interfere or influence your child's enjoyment of it.

-Mention who the composer is and act out the instruments as you hear them played.

-Swoosh scarves around as you dance to music.

-Use puppets or stuffed animals to dance to music.

-Paint, color, or felt pen to music. (See "Paint to Music" in chap. 4.)

-Get a light-weight, brightly colored tablecloth. Take one end, holding the two corners. Let your child take the other two. When the music goes up, pull the tablecloth up like a parachute. When the music goes down low, let the tablecloth float down.

-Play "Flight of the Bumblebee" and act like bees!

-Clap, step, click tongue, jump, swing arms, to the music's beat.

-Does the music make you happy? Sad? Let's make up a happy dance, a sad dance, an angry dance, a sleepy dance.

-While using small ropes (approximately 3 feet long), make shapes and designs while listening to music.

-Get a pillow and close your eyes while listening to music. It's a nice time to snuggle!

-Play records by Hap Palmer (see Resources) or other children's music artists that encourage children to participate with the music.

-Use rhythm instruments to play along with all kinds of music. They can be purchased in toy and educational supply stores or can be made. Here are a few ideas to use with rhythm instruments:

- Play your instrument up high, down low, to the side, behind you, between your legs, in front of you.
- March, skip, run, and jump playing your instruments.
- Beat rhythm sticks, drums, etc., to the beat of "Yankee Doodle," "Hickory Dickory Dock," or some other song with a strong beat.
- Play your instrument fast, slow, hard, soft.
- Use instruments to illustrate sounds that might occur in a story that you're reading—clicking sounds for rain or insects, sand blocks for ocean waves or wind blowing, tinkling sounds for growing plants, coconut shells for running horses.
- Or simply play instruments to favorite songs.

Easy Rhythm Instruments to Make

Many preschool rhythm instruments are inexpensive enough to buy, but the following can be made from household items:*

Rhythm sticks
-Doweling. Paint them. Buy doweling with ridges for a variety in sound when two are rubbed together. Run a comb over the ribbing for still another sound.

-Chopsticks or well-cleaned rib bones can be used for rhythm sticks. Sand and paint them if desired.

-Bang paper towel tubing together.

Rattles
-Spice tins filled with sand, dried beans, rice, or rocks.

-Toilet paper tubes filled with beans or rocks. Put tape over the ends.

-Poke a hole in a hollow gourd, large enough to put beans, barley, or rice into. Tape over hole.

-Hollow plastic eggs or any container with a lid. Fill with beans, etc. Tape lid or egg halves together.

Drum
-Oatmeal tubs. Nothing has to be done except to tape the lid on. The top can be beaten with hands or spoons. Paint or cover with gift wrap or patterned contact paper.

*Many thanks to Annette Peck for her creative input into this section.

Bangers
-Pot lids or pot and pot lid together make a fine, LOUD sound!

-Metal pie plates. Bang with spoons or tap with fingers.

Coconut shells
-Saw in half for *clopping* sounds.

Sand blocks
-Glue or thumbtack sandpaper onto one side of two squares of wood. Rub together. Turn them over and bang the bare wood sides against each other.

Grater
Run a plastic spoon or comb over a cheese grater for scratching sounds.

Triangle
-Large nail tied at head with lacing. Tap with another nail for triangle sound.

-Hang horseshoe with string. Strike with wrench or large nail.

Spoons
-Bang together or hang with string and strike.

Tooter
-Toilet paper tube to use like a kazoo.

Bells
-Attach a string to jingle the bells or attach bells to a tea strainer. Add ribbon for decoration.

Fun instruments to buy are a whistle or a kazoo. Also, see Resources for a few suggestions in children's records.

A TIME TO SERVE

19
Cooking

What fun you'll have cooking together! Remember to be patient and don't rush. Depending on your child's age, you may have to help him do almost every step, but as he sees a process through from beginning to end, he will have great satisfaction and pride in his efforts—and his love for cooking will continue to grow.

Cooking is also an avenue for emphasizing hospitality. Through cooking for others he learns to serve others—to think of others before himself. He learns that making a food pleasing to look at is serving someone too. Through cooking for fun, a child will:

-Learn to enjoy cooking

-See a process from beginning to end

-Learn the value of food

-Learn about all types of food and where they come from

-Learn what is good and bad for his body

-Develop a liking for many foods

-Learn what a recipe is

-Learn specific names of cooking utensils and ingredients

-Learn what specific ingredients taste like

-Learn the importance of clean hands when cooking and when eating

-Learn to help clean the kitchen afterward

WHAT CAN WE START WITH?

Stirring
Making Popsicles and ice cubes
Cracking eggs
Cutting soft bananas, biscuits, etc., with blunt knife
Spreading mayonnaise, butter, jam, peanut butter, frosting
Decorating cookies and cupcakes

EDIBLE INSECTS

Supplies needed:
celery stalk
peanut butter
raisins
4 stick pretzels
Cut celery stalk to desired insect length. Fill with peanut butter. Lay pretzel sticks across stalk for legs. Add raisin eyes, and break one pretzel stick in half for antennae.

FROZEN BANANAS

Supplies needed:
bananas
can of chocolate syrup
tongue depressor or Popsicle stick
chopped nuts
Cut banana in half crossways. Insert stick into end of each half. Dip banana in chocolate syrup and roll in nuts. Freeze on cookie sheet.

COOKIE PAINT

Supplies needed:
- 2 egg yolks
- 1 T. water
- food coloring
- containers for colors

Mix the egg yolks and water well. Divide into separate containers and add food coloring. Apply to unbaked cookie thickly with paint brush. Bake cookie according to recipe instructions.

The following recipes are creations of Mary Buckman of Mary Bee Creations. I want to thank her for her willingness to share them with us! (See Resources for ordering her cookbooks.)

ELEPHANT EAR MIXTURE

Supplies needed:
- ⅓ c. flour
- 2 tsp. baking powder
- 1 tsp. baking soda
- ½ tsp. salt

Mix well. Pour into a bowl, ready for children to scoop out. (See p. 111 for use.)

MONSTER MUFFINS MIXTURE

Supplies needed:
- ⅔ c. whole wheat flour
- 2 T. brown sugar
- 1½ tsp. baking powder
- ¼ tsp. salt

Mix thoroughly and pour into a bowl ready for children to scoop out. Makes 5-6 muffins. (See p. 121 for further instructions.)

tiger paws

Get **1** biscuit

Cut into 3 pieces

Shape into short fat pieces

Push the pieces together into a "paw"

Count **3** almond "claws"

Push the "claws" into the paw, and sprinkle with sugar and cinnamon

Bake 450° 10 min.

hairy harvey

Get a slice of bread

Cut a circle face

Get another slice of bread

Cut another circle. Then cut it in half

Make the circles into a rabbit. Frost with soft butter

Decorate with mini-marshmallow cheeks, fruit eyes and tongue, coconut hair and licorice string whiskers

bev's crocodile carrots

Get
a carrot

Ask a grown-up
to please cut
the mouth out

Count
two raisins
for eyes

"Glue"
the eyes on
with peanut butter

Get
some slivered almonds
for teeth

"Glue"
the teeth inside
the mouth
with peanut butter

owl-bert

Get a slice of bread

Spread butter or cheese spread on the bread

Slice a hard-boiled egg to make "owl eyes"

Cut cheese for ears, nose, and feet!

elephant ears

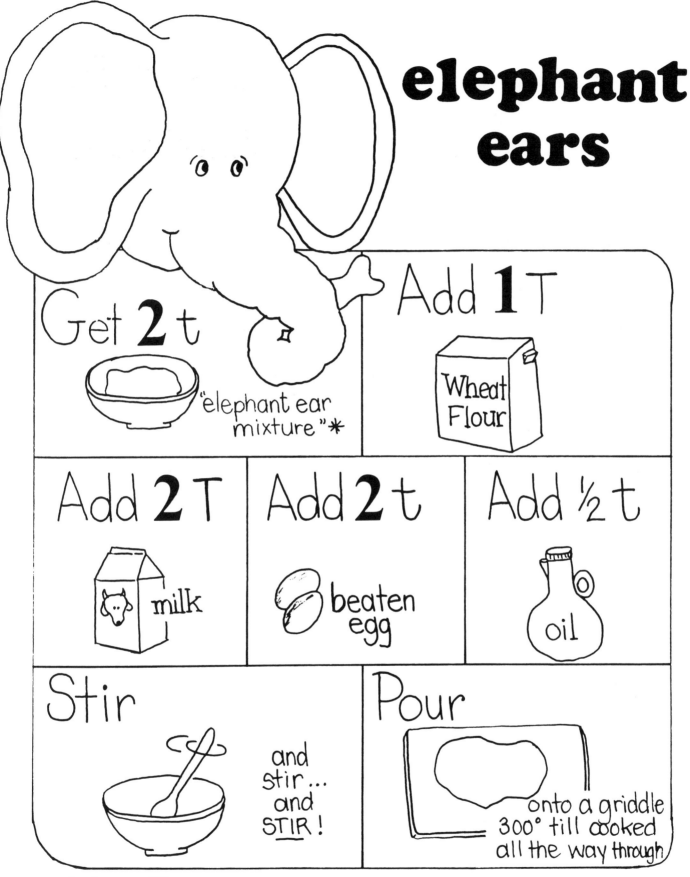

Get **2** t
"elephant ear mixture"*

Add **1** T
Wheat Flour

Add **2** T
milk

Add **2** t
beaten egg

Add ½ t
oil

Stir
and stir... and S<u>TIR</u>!

Pour
onto a griddle 300° till cooked all the way through

*recipe on p. 106

crawly critter

Get ½ banana

Peel the banana

Cut a few banana circles

Dip the circles in different kinds of cookie sprinkles

Put the circles together

Add raisin, nut or candy eyes and licorice feelers

brown bear

Get a ball of brown bear dough* and make a big bear tummy

Roll a medium-sized ball of dough and make a head

Roll four little balls for arms and legs

Add two tiny little balls for ears

Decorate with nuts and raisins

Bake 350° on a little piece of foil 15 min.

*recipe for dough p. 114

Brown Bear

Shopping List

- foil
- nuts
- raisins
- "brown bear dough"

Brown Bear Dough:
Cream 1/3 c shortening, 1½ c molasses, and 1 c brown sugar. Add 2/3 c cold water. Add 2t soda 1t salt, 1t allspice, 1t ginger, 1t cinnamon. Blend in 6 c flour. Knead, and divide into balls of dough for the children to shape!
Makes 15 or 20

Animal Art

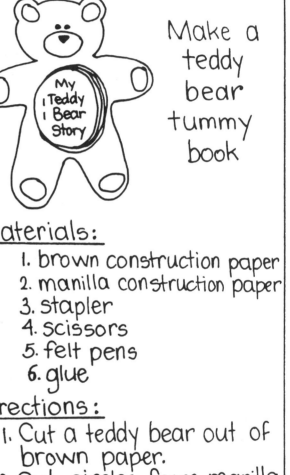

Make a teddy bear tummy book

Materials:
1. brown construction paper
2. manilla construction paper
3. stapler
4. scissors
5. felt pens
6. glue

Directions:
1. Cut a teddy bear out of brown paper.
2. Cut circles from manilla paper to trim paws and ears and face.
3. Cut several tummies and make it into a storybook.

mister monkey

Cut a circle face from a slice of bread

Get another slice of bread

Cut a circle for a muzzle and two little circles for ears

Spread peanut butter on the face and ears

Put the muzzle on the face

Decorate the face with raisins, nuts, sunflower seeds

115

prickly porcupine

Get a biscuit dough

Count 7 pretzels

Break the pretzels in half and push hard into the biscuit

Push two peanut eyes into your porcupine

Bake 450° 10 min.

116

alvin allosaurus

Cut a thick slice of bread in half

Spread soft cream cheese on both halves

Put the halves together and push a few cucumber slices in the spine

Cut a piece of velveeta cheese for a head, and give it nut or raisin eyes

Push a thin slice of celery into the cheese

Push the neck into the body

hash-brown harry

Grate
half of a small potato

Squish
it into a circle

Cook
in a little oil for 7 min. 350°

Turn
and cook the other side 7 min.

Decorate
with cheese eyes, a raisin nose...

And
a big ketchup smile

ketchup

wilbur whale

Get a MINI-french roll

Ask a grown-up please to cut out two triangles to make a tail.

Spread your favorite filling inside

Cut carrots into little pieces for teeth and fins

Count two olives for eyes

Put it all together

munchy mouse

Get a scoop of ice cream. Put it in a cupcake paper

Push vanilla wafers into the ice cream for ears

Push raisins or peanuts into the ice cream for eyes

Add a long licorice string tail

monster muffins

Get **2** T
monster muffin mixture*

Add **1** T
Corn Meal

Add **1** T
Milk

Add **1** T
beaten egg

Add **1** T
oil

Stir
and scoop into a cupcake paper

Bake 400° 15 min

Decorate
with frosting or...
...peanut butter, pretzels, fruit, nuts, popcorn, candy, and pipe cleaners!

121

*monster muffin batter p. 106

little lamb

Count 5 T

whipped cream on a piece of waxed paper

Stir

the cream around and make a little lamb

Cover

the cream with coconut "lamb's wool" and add raisin eyes.

Freeze

overnight... Then peel off the waxed paper!

lifesaver lollipop

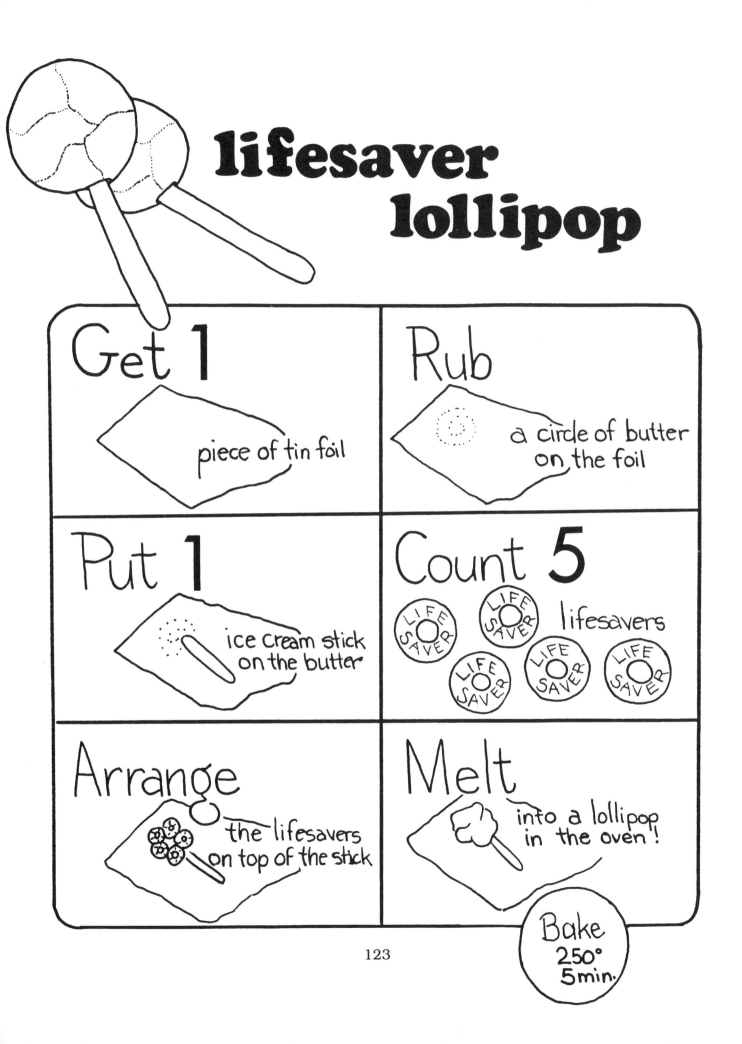

Get 1 piece of tin foil

Rub a circle of butter on the foil

Put 1 ice cream stick on the butter

Count 5 lifesavers

Arrange the lifesavers on top of the stick

Melt into a lollipop in the oven!

Bake 250° 5 min.

A TIME TO TRAVEL

20
Outings

Each town, city, or suburb has its own unique places to offer children. Below are some ideas to consider for your area. For more suggestions, contact your chamber of commerce or a nearby university that has a child development department. Even a local preschool might have helpful hints to offer.

-Visit city playgrounds.

-Feed the ducks at the park and have a picnic.

-Enjoy city wading pool.

-If a nearby university has an agricultural department, they may allow you to visit the farm animals being raised there.

-Is there a science center in town where hands-on and/or observation experiences are offered?

-Does your zoo have a science program for children? Often in these classes children are also involved in art, cooking, and puppetry.

-Take escalator or elevator rides in department stores.

-Visit museums.

-Take your car through a car wash while you stay inside the car.

-Art centers: Many art centers have exhibitions or rooms especially designed to interest children.

-Visit railroad station or take a short ride on the train.

-Go to airport.

-Is there a mall where children's art or other exhibits of interest might be displayed?

-Take a ride to the country for a picnic.

-Visit a fowl or fish hatchery.

-Visit a dairy.

-Take a trip to a rabbit or turkey farm.

-Visit a healthy, elderly friend or relative.

-Go watch construction work where tractors are being used.

-Take a bus ride.

-Visit a fire station (call ahead).

-Go get an ice cream cone!

-Visit a pet shop or aquarium store. Look for the Kissing Gouramis! Are there any saltwater tanks to view?

-Visit fountains or statues.

-Is there a dam to visit?

-Go to vacation Bible school.

-Library: Libraries have wonderful children's departments and offer many activities including a story time, art activities, movies, and puppet shows (especially during summer months).

-Go to see an animal shelter.

-Visit a factory nearby (call ahead).

-Go roller skating (if you're not a roller skater, just walk alongside your child).

-Visit a water slide!

-Watch large road machinery at work.

-Visit a pumpkin patch.

-Play miniature golf (children five and under are often free).

21
When Traveling with a Young Child

Although the ideas below are meant for long distance traveling, many can be applied to the short trip in town. The suggestions in the next chapter for a sick child are also applicable. Look over both sections before buckling them up.

-Take along hand or finger puppets.

-Put away toys your child doesn't play with very often and use them only for car trips.

-Stop every hour for ten minutes of running, jumping, and potty breaks. Your trip may be a little longer, but it will be much more enjoyable.

-Have a surprise, inexpensive toy every hour for the duration of the trip. Three-through five-year-olds enjoy small, rubbery animals or Gumby-like characters to play with. Hobby shops have small Christmas ornaments or little birds, and so on, for play.

-A rectangular cake pan with a slide lid makes a terrific desk for a child able to use a regular seat belt. Crayons, books, writing pad, and small toys can be stored inside the pan. The lid doubles as a table top for drawing or as a playing surface.

-Take along new books.

-Bring library books.

-Bring a doll cut-out on a shoe box (see chap. 15).

-Supply small magnetic board games from the dime store.

-Let him play with a kaleidoscope.

-Give him a hand mirror.

-Fill a bag with odds and ends from your junk drawer (including kitchen gadgets).

-Play children's songs and/or stories on tape. Many storybooks come with tapes.* If you don't have a car tape deck, bring along a portable one.

-Play tape of family events or recordings of child's first talking.

-Sing together. Say nursery rhymes.

-Have an unusual, surprise snack or lunch.

-Bring along a small flannelboard for making up stories and rhymes (see chap. 14).

-Colorforms and Etch-A-Sketch are fun toys for the car.

-Talk about what you are seeing along the way, noticing shapes, colors, and listening to sounds. Name objects as you notice them.

-View Masters make fun travel toys. These are the binocular-type viewers with the circular slides. There is a tremendous assortment of stories and characters available.

---

*You can make your own story tapes by recording one of your child's books. Preschoolers need a signal for turning the pages, so ring a bell, bang a pot lid, or simply tell them to turn the page. Talk slowly. When you are ready to travel, be sure to bring the book along.

-Give them stickers and a small writing pad or sticker book. They will enjoy putting the stickers onto the pages and then "reading" their book!

-If you can take the noise, why not have a bag of rhythm instruments to play while you all sing together? Fisher-Price has a wonderful put-together instrument called Crazy Combo Horn Set, or just bring a xylophone!

A TIME TO REST

22
When Your Child Is Sick

A preschooler usually cannot stay in bed, but here are a few ideas to make his illness a special time for both of you.

Meals:

-Put each part of his meal into small paper bags. Ask him to guess what is in each bag by smelling and feeling.

-Cut toast, sandwiches, Jello into various shapes: circle, triangle, rabbit, star.

-Make food a surprise, such as Elephant Ears for breakfast or Hairy Harvey for lunch (see chap. 19).

-Make orange juice Popsicles to keep liquids in him. Add plain gelatin to give protein to the Popsicles.

Activities:

-A shoe box filled with crayons, paper, blunt childrens' scissors to keep on the nightstand

-Books (New ones are a treat to look at, and later on Mom can come and snuggle up and read them aloud. Library books are just as good!)

-Hand and finger puppets (see chap. 16)

-A stuffed toy to hug

-A softly played tape of children's songs and/or stories

-A tape of your child's voice and/or family voices from past tape-recorded events

-Small pinball or magnetic games from the dime store

-A sack of safe, unusual kitchen gadgets

-Going through the family album together

-Having him dictate a one-sentence letter to a relative or a friend

-A safe, plastic see-through music box

-Stringing macaroni or beads

-An inexpensive new toy (a little bird from the hobby shop or an old typewriter ribbon cartridge for a space ship)

-Play dough in a large roasting pan or lap TV tray

-A kaleidoscope

-A flannelboard with felt cutouts or a magnet board with shapes, letters

Atmosphere:

-Hang a mobile above the bed.

-Hang posters or magazine pictures on ceiling or near pillow.

-Do as many chores as you can in is room (ironing, washing his window, mending, etc.).

-Play his favorite music softly.

A TIME TO RENEW

23
Special Days

Every once in a while we all need a pick-me-up, and what better way than to have a special day in your neighborhood—parents and children! Build on the suggestions here, and make your own event extra special.

Rainbow Day: Paint with all the colors of the rainbow. Decorate cookies with colored sprinkles. Wear different colors of clothing and blow colored bubbles (see chap. 13). Make a rainbow with a garden hose (see chap. 10). Paint rainbows on cheeks with liquid tempera paint and liquid dish soap.

Pet Day: Have neighborhood friends bring pets together for a pet show. Each can tell how he cares for his pet. Eat animal crackers and drink moose juice (any kind of juice).

Oriental Meal: Have each child bring part of a Chinese meal and sit on the floor to eat it. Be sure to take off shoes. Plastic tablecloths or butcher paper make a fine table for kids. Check out Oriental music at the library to play while you eat.

Pool Day: Neighbors bring their wading pools to your backyard and let the kids enjoy. Fill one pool with soap bubbles, another colored with food coloring, and leave another clear. Snack might be Popsicles and fruit slices with orange juice.

Art Exhibit: From his art box, your child can choose art representative of various types of media (painting, gluing, 3-D art, etc.). Set up in your backyard by tacking to fence or posts, or in one room of your house. Have neighborhood friends bring their art to display and invite all parents to come view the masterpieces.

Carnival Day: Set up backyard into separate events (swings, slide, bars, obstacle course, painting faces, bean bag toss, etc.). Each child is given tickets and can do whatever he wishes. Parents man each activity. Decorate with balloons and streamers. Have a table set up for one-ticket snacks. You might even want to set up simple games to win sticker prizes.

A Parade: A parade of anything—trikes, wagons, dolls, hats, different shoes, kazoos, puppets, rhythm instruments.

Thanksgiving Feast: A week before Thanksgiving (when you still have some time!) let the kids help make a crock-pot of "Thankful Stew." Each child contributes a vegetable and helps prepare it for the pot. When done, invite everyone to sit down and tell one thing they are thankful for. Say a blessing and dig in! You might want to let the children make Indian headbands and/or pilgrim hats.

Crazy Day: Wear mismatched clothing, eat a light dinner at breakfast time and a breakfast at dinnertime. Eat on the floor or with your chairs turned sideways. Do a crazy junk-art type activity and bang rhythm instruments in a parade.

Pumpkin Day: As an alternative to witches and goblins, have a pumpkin party. Have each child, with his parents, bring one small pumpkin and a knife. Beforehand, you and your children make pumpkin-shaped cookies, punch to serve in a hollowed out pumpkin, a simple paper "Pin the Nose on the Pumpkin" game, and paper pumpkin seeds for a pumpkin seed hunt. At the party, the kids decorate their cookies, carve out their pumpkins with their parents, go on a seed hunt for a special sweet treat (raisins, fruit roll, etc.), and play "Pin the Nose on the Pumpkin"! Involve the parents in each activity.

A TIME FOR CAUTION

24
Choosing a Quality Preschool

Many working mothers are seeking full-time quality child care whereas others want a twice-a-week, half-day enrichment program, purely for their child's socialization. Whatever your situation and needs, you must be particular. Don't assume that because it is a school for children that it's the right school for your child. Here are some things to look for (and to ask directors and teachers) before enrolling your child:

1. Look around at *all* the schools in your area.
2. Spend as much time observing the schools as possible before deciding. Be sensitive to any hesititation on the school's part to let you observe. A quality school will encourage visitation any time.
3. Does the school offer enrichment? What kind?
   a. Do the activities provided allow for self-expression, or are the outcomes teacher-determined?
   b. Is the curriculum overly structured? (Children are not free to play if they don't want to do art, for example.)
   c. Is the curriculum totally unstructured? (Little or no activities offered.)
   d. Or is the curriculum a happy medium of free-flowing activities and choices that the children can make?
4. Are there definite areas for play (playhouse, block area, manipulative toy area, book area, science area). Preschools in homes are often not able to have definite areas, but this does not take away from the quality offered there.
5. Are the toys on the shelves actually used by the children, or are they just for show? (Yes, this *is* what happens in a few schools.) By observing an entire morning, you can determine things like this.
6. Does the school allow for privacy for children? (Quiet, cozy area for reading, quiet conversations, and relaxation.)
7. What is the child-teacher ratio? (Twelve to one is the law in California. What is it in your state? This ratio should not include any staff member who is not a teacher, such as a cook or bus driver).
8. How is dicipline handled? Do the teachers handle the children with firmness yet with positive language and dignity?
9. Do the teachers seem to know and care about the children?
10. Do the children seem happy?
11. What is the general atmosphere?
12. Are the teachers willing to work with parents on allergy problems?
13. Is proper sleeping equipment provided for naptime? (Cots, fairly dark room, teachers present with the children to comfort them.)
14. Are hot lunches served? Are they nutritious? Ask for that month's menu.
15. Does the playground offer a variety of areas—sand, grass, dirt, wood chips? Each is important to children's play.
16. Does the equipment allow for creativity in play, or is it simply "cute" equipment to please parents' eyes?

143

17. Does the school provide monthly in-service training for its teachers?

18. What are the teachers' qualifications? Must they have taken several child development classes as a minimum requirement? This is very important because it affects the quality of child-teacher interaction and quality of the enrichment program.

19. Do the teachers have weekly staff meetings? Staff meetings are important because the children's needs and the program needs are discussed there.

20. Are parent conferences available by request?

There are so many things to look for, but your child is worth it! Some of the above will not pertain to small, home preschools, but you still need to spend plenty of time observing, noting even whether the furniture is safe for children playing near. The more established preschools, large or small, should be able to meet almost all of the above. These guidelines are to help you evaluate what you see. If parents would select their schools carefully, the schools that are not offering quality child care and enrichment would soon be forced to do so.

A TIME FOR REFLECTION

25

In closing, I'd like to share a poem that has meant a great deal to me. It isn't meant to create guilt feelings, but instead, to serve as a reminder to both of us that the time spent with our children is precious!

I WISH . . .

The room is neat, without a sound
And lonely as I look around
Remembering yet another day
You wanted me to stop and play.

But I was busy, with things to do
I didn't have much time for you
Or the verse you wanted me to hear—
And my reply was, "Later dear."

My days were full of busy tasks
No time for questions that you asked

You wanted to share the things you'd learned
But when you looked my back was turned.

The years rush by, I wish I'd known
That you would be so quickly grown
No longer holding out to me
The need I was too rushed to see.

And now the toys are put away
We've no more songs or games to play
No goodnight kiss or stories to hear—
That's all a part of another year.

I wish I could go back again
Relive those years as they might have been
And the little things you asked me to do
I wish I'd made more time for you.

(Author Unknown)

God bless you and your children as you grow, play, and experience together in your special bond of love.

Reflections

The following blank pages are provided to you for reflecting on your experiences, thoughts, reactions, and feelings during the activities with your children.

Resources

BOOKS ON PARENT-CHILD RELATIONSHIPS

Campbell, Ross. *How to Really Love Your Child.* Wheaton, Ill.: Scripture Press, Victor, 1977.

Ortlund, Anne. *Children Are Wet Cement.* Old Tappan, N.J.: Revell, 1978.

Swindoll, Charles R. *You and Your Child.* Nashville: Nelson, 1977.

DEVOTIONAL BOOKS FOR LITTLE ONES

Beers, V. Gilbert. *My Picture Bible to See and Share.* Wheaton, Ill.: Scripture Press, Victor, 1982.

Charette, Beverly Rae. *Christian Nursery Rhymes.* Nashville: Ideals, 1982.

Coleman, William L. *Before You Tuck Me In.* Minneapolis: Bethany House, 1985.

—————. *The Good Night Book.* Minneapolis: Bethany House, 1979.

—————. *The Sleep Tight Book.* Minneapolis: Bethany House, 1982.

Hunter, Emily. *The Bible Time Nursery Rhyme Book.* Eugene, Ore.: Harvest House, 1984.

—————. *Little Lips Shall Praise Thee.* Harvest House, 1986.

Jahsmann, Alan Hart, and Simon, Martin P. *Little Visits with God.* St. Louis: Concordia, 1957.

—————. *More Little Visits with God.* St. Louis: Concordia, 1961.

Lindvall, Ella K. *The Bible Illustrated for Little Children.* Chicago: Moody, 1985.

—————. *Read Aloud Bible Stories*, vol. 1. Chicago: Moody, 1982.

—————. *Read Aloud Bible Stories*, vol. 2. Chicago: Moody, 1985.

Mason, Alice Leedy. *Christian Bedtime Rhymes.* Nashville: Ideals, 1984.

Taylor, Kenneth N. *The Bible in Pictures for Little Eyes.* Chicago: Moody, 1956, 1985.

—————. *Big Thoughts for Little People.* Wheaton, Ill.: Tyndale, 1983.

—————. *Giant Steps for Little People.* Wheaton, Ill.: Tyndale, 1985.

CHARACTER BUILDING/CHRISTIAN VALUES

Agapeland Character Builders stories and tapes (Sparrow Records, Birdwing).

Critter County Storytime series (stories and cassettes) from Standard Publishing.

Barrett, Ethel. *Communicating Christian Values to Children* series (stories and tapes). Glendale, Calif.: Gospel Light, Regal Books.

Happy Day Books (Cincinnati: Standard Publishing).

Murphy, Elspeth Campbell. *David and I Talk to God* series. Elgin, Ill.: David C. Cook, Chariot Books.

—————. *God's Word in My Heart* series. Elgin, Ill.: David C. Cook, Chariot Books.

SCIENCE RESOURCES

Your Big Backyard (magazine for preschoolers)
National Wildlife Federation
1412 16th St. N.W.
Washington, D.C. 20036

World Magazine (for elementary age)
National Geographic Society
P.O. Box 2330
Washington, D.C. 20013

Ranger Rick Magazine (for elementary age)
National Wildlife Federation
1412 16th St. N.W.
Washington, D.C. 20036

Insect Lore Products
P.O. Box 1535
Shafter, CA 93263
(Ask for catalog for nature kits.)

Concepts

Sesame Street Magazine
P.O. Box 2896
Boulder, CO 80322

The Electric Company (magazine for elementary age)
200 Watt Street
P.O. Box 51277
Boulder, CO

Cooking Resource

Mary Bee Creations
24 East 25th Ave.
San Mateo, CA 94403

(Ask for information on the *Animal Cookbook* and the *Count and Cook Book*.)

Puppetry Resources

Nancy Renfro Studios
1117 W. 9th St.
Austin, TX 78703
(Ask for information on the book *Puppetry in Early Childhood Education*.)

Rottman, Fran. *Easy to Make Puppets and How to Use Them.* Glendale, Calif.: Gospel Light, Regal, 1978.

Fingerplays and Records

Hap Palmer activity records. For a free catalog write to Educational Activities, Inc., Freeport, NY 11520

Kid's Sing Praise (tape)—familiar favorite Christian children's songs (Brentwood Records).

Music Machines' Agapeland album series (Sparrow Records, Birdwing).

Praise and *Kids' Praise* album series (Word Records, Maranatha Music).

Beall, Pamela Conn, and Nipp, Susan Hagen. *Wee Sing* (music book includes fingerplays and a tape). Los Angeles: Price, Stern, Sloan, 1985.

—————. *Wee Sing Silly Songs.* Los Angeles: Price, Stern, Sloan, 1977.

Moody Press, a ministry of the Moody Bible Institute, is designed for education, evangelization, and edification. If we may assist you in knowing more about Christ and the Christian life, please write us without obligation: Moody Press, c/o MLM, Chicago, Illinois 60610.